HOK

A Global Design Portfolio

In memoriam

"We're a firm that's not afraid to lead. We never have been. We know we won't be following in anyone's path. Our hallmark has always been the ability to veer off the comfortable road, to go after new service offerings, new locations, and markets. Forging our own path is much more difficult than following.

It takes courage, passion, knowledge, and imagination. But having the opportunity to redefine not only what we do, but the entire profession, is immensely more exciting than simply following."

John Mahon
1946–2008

h+k

HOK

A Global Design Portfolio

images
Publishing

Published in Australia in 2009 by
The Images Publishing Group Pty Ltd
ABN 89 059 734 431
6 Bastow Place, Mulgrave, Victoria 3170, Australia
Tel: +61 3 9561 5544 Fax: +61 3 9561 4860
books@imagespublishing.com
www.imagespublishing.com

Copyright © The Images Publishing Group Pty Ltd 2009
The Images Publishing Group Reference Number: 808

National Library of Australia Cataloguing-in-Publication entry

Title: HOK : a global design portfolio.

ISBN: 9781864703146 (hbk.)

Subjects: Hellmuth, Obata & Kassabaum.
                    Architecture, American.
                    Architecture, Modern–20th century.
                    Architecture, Modern–21st century.
                    Architecture–Environmental aspects.
                    Architecture and energy conservation.

Dewey Number: 720.973

Coordinating editor: Robyn Beaver

Design concept: Jim Doussard, HOK

Production by The Graphic Image Studio Pty Ltd, Mulgrave, Australia
www.tgis.com.au

Digital production by Chroma Graphics (Overseas) Pte Ltd, Singapore
Printed on FSC-certified paper by Everbest Printing Co. Ltd., in Hong Kong/China

Mixed Sources
Product group from well-managed
forests, and other controlled sources
www.fsc.org Cert no. SGS-COC-003563
© 1996 Forest Stewardship Council
FSC

Contents

The Architecture Firm of the Future   9
by Hilary Lewis

Selected Projects

40 Peak Road Residential Development   14
Hong Kong, China

150 California   18
San Francisco, California, USA

Accenture Offices   22
Seattle, Washington, USA

AGL Resources Headquarters Renovation   26
Atlanta, Georgia, USA

Alfred A. Arraj United States Courthouse   28
Denver, Colorado, USA

Allsteel Resource Center Showroom and Offices   32
Atlanta, Georgia and Boston, Massachusetts, USA

America Online Regional Headquarters   36
Beverly Hills, California, USA

Amsterdam Passenger Terminal   40
Amsterdam, The Netherlands

Anaheim Convention Center   44
Anaheim, California, USA

Barclays Bank Headquarters   48
London, UK

Barnes-Jewish Hospital Center for Advanced Medicine   54
St. Louis, Missouri, USA

Barranca del Muerto 329   58
Mexico City, Mexico

Biogen Idec Campus   60
San Diego, California, USA

Bladensburg High School   66
Bladensburg, Maryland, USA

Boeing Leadership Center Campus and Carriage House   70
St. Louis, Missouri, USA

Capital One Canada Offices   74
North York, Ontario, Canada

Central Japan International Airport (Chubu Centrair) Terminal   76
Tokoname City, Aichi, Japan

Chevy Chase Center   80
Chevy Chase, Maryland, USA

Children's Discovery Museum   84
San José, California, USA

Cisco Systems Executive Briefing Center   88
San José, California, USA

Ciudad Mitras Master Plan   92
Monterrey, Mexico

Community Hospital of the Monterey Peninsula   94
Monterey, California, USA

Community of Christ World Headquarters   96
Independence, Missouri, USA

Confluence Greenway and Great Rivers Greenway Master Plan   98
St. Louis, Missouri, USA

Cork International Airport Passenger Terminal   102
Cork, Ireland

Crystal Tower   108
Kuwait City, Kuwait

The Darwin Centre Phase One at The Natural History Museum   112
London, UK

Dasve Village Master Plan, Lavasa Hill Station   118
Maharashtra, India

Dechert LLP Law Offices   122
London, UK

Dubai Marina Master Plan   126
Dubai, United Arab Emirates

East Taihu Lake Waterfront District   130
Wujiang, China

Edificio Malecon Office Tower   132
Buenos Aires, Argentina

Emerson Grand Basin / *Post-Dispatch* Lake in Forest Park   136
St. Louis, Missouri, USA

Federal Reserve Bank of Cleveland Headquarters Expansion and Renovation   140
Cleveland, Ohio, USA

Federal Reserve Bank of Minneapolis Headquarters and Operations Center   144
Minneapolis, Minnesota, USA

Florida Aquarium   146
Tampa, Florida, USA

Contents

Florida International University Patricia & Philip Frost Art Museum   148
Miami, Florida, USA

Foreign & Commonwealth Office, Whitehall   152
London, UK

Forest Park Jewel Box Grounds   156
St. Louis, Missouri, USA

40 Grosvenor Place   158
London, UK

Franchise Tax Board Offices   162
Sacramento, California, USA

Fukuoka International Airport International Passenger Terminal   164
Fukuoka, Japan

Georgia Archives   168
Morrow, Georgia, USA

Guy Carpenter Headquarters   172
New York, New York, USA

Hampton Roads Convention Center   176
Hampton, Virginia, USA

Harlem Hospital Center Master Plan and Patient Pavilion   180
New York, New York, USA

Indianapolis International Airport Col. H. Weir Cook Terminal   182
Indianapolis, Indiana, USA

James J. Stukel Towers and UIC Forum – University of Illinois   186
Chicago, Illinois, USA

JWT Offices   190
Chicago, Illinois, USA

Kai Tak Archipelago Master Plan   194
Hong Kong, China

Kellogg Corporate Headquarters   196
Battle Creek, Michigan, USA

Kent County Courthouse   198
Warwick, Rhode Island, USA

Kiener Plaza   200
St. Louis, Missouri, USA

Killbear Provincial Park Visitor Centre   204
Noble, Ontario, Canada

King Abdullah University of Science and Technology   210
Rabigh, Saudi Arabia

King's Library at the British Museum   216
London, UK

Kingwood College Health & Science Building   218
Kingwood, Texas, USA

London Marriott West India Quay Tower   222
London, UK

Maricopa County Fourth Avenue Jail   226
Phoenix, Arizona, USA

MasterCard Global Technology and Operations Headquarters   228
O'Fallon, Missouri, USA

McGuire Woods LLP Law Offices   230
Century City, California, USA

MedImmune Research and Office Campus   232
Gaithersburg, Maryland, USA

Missouri Historical Society Expansion and Renovation   236
St. Louis, Missouri, USA

Motorola Executive Offices Renovation   240
Schaumburg, Illinois, USA

National Air and Space Museum   242
Washington, DC, USA

National Air and Space Museum Steven F. Udvar-Hazy Center   246
Chantilly, Virginia, USA

National Wildlife Federation Headquarters   252
Reston, Virginia, USA

New Doha International Airport   254
Doha, Qatar

NOAA Center for Weather and Climate Prediction   258
Riverdale Park, Maryland, USA

Nortel Brampton Centre   260
Brampton, Ontario, Canada

Ogilvy & Mather Offices   262
Chicago, Illinois, USA

The Ohio State University Medical Center   266
Columbus, Ohio, USA

One McKinley Place   268
Makati, Philippines

Orange County Groundwater Replenishment System   270
Orange County, California, USA

Pole Project
Moscow, Russia
274

The Priory Chapel
St. Louis, Missouri, USA
280

Reforma 27 Tower
Mexico City, Mexico
284

St. Barnabas Church
Dulwich, UK
286

St. George Intermodal and Cultural Center
Staten Island, New York, USA
288

St. Louis County Memorial Plaza
Clayton, Missouri, USA
292

St. Louis Mississippi Riverfront Master Plan
St. Louis, Missouri, USA
296

Salvador Dali Museum
St. Petersburg, Florida, USA
298

Sam M. Gibbons U.S. Courthouse
Tampa, Florida, USA
302

Samsung Research and Development Campus
Suwon, South Korea
304

San Bernardino Natural Sciences Annex California State University
San Bernardino, California, USA
310

San Mateo County Sheriff's Forensic Laboratory and Coroner's Office
San Mateo, California, USA
314

Sanya Haitang Bay National Seashore Master Plan
Hainan, China
316

Sheraton Timika Eco-Hotel
Timika, Irian Jaya, Indonesia
318

SJ Berwin LLP Offices
London, UK
322

Symantec Executive Boardroom
Cupertino, California, USA
328

Time Inc. Conference Center
New York, New York, USA
330

Tokyo Telecom Center
Tokyo, Japan
334

Tyson Foods Discovery Center
Springdale, Arkansas, USA
338

University Health Network Toronto Hospital New Clinical Services Building 342
Toronto, Ontario, Canada

The University of Houston-Clear Lake Student Services Building
Clear Lake, Texas, USA
344

U.S. Department of State Nairobi Embassy Compound
Nairobi, Kenya
346

U.S. Department of State New Office Building
Moscow, Russia
350

U.S. EPA Environmental Research Center
Research Triangle Park, North Carolina, USA
356

USAA Phoenix Norterra Campus
Phoenix, Arizona, USA
360

Warner Music Canada Headquarters
Markham, Ontario, Canada
364

William Rainey Harper College Avanté Center
Palatine, Illinois, USA
368

WilTel Technology Center Headquarters
Tulsa, Oklahoma, USA
372

Winrock International Headquarters
Little Rock, Arkansas, USA
376

Zayed University
Dubai, United Arab Emirates
380

Zentrum Tower
Mexico City, Mexico
386

Firm Credits

Executive Committee
393

HOK Board of Directors 2008–2009
394

Design Leaders
396

HOK Employees 2008
403

HOK Global Office Locations
412

Photography and Illustration Credits
413

The Architecture Firm of the Future

After more than 50 years of practice, HOK has achieved an estimable place in the profession of architecture. Now a firm that exceeds 2,500 professionals with 26 offices worldwide, it has the ability to tackle the most complex, geographically diverse, and technically advanced projects imaginable. But HOK has not been content to rest at this level; it has actively worked to reinvent itself—continuously—not just by growing larger, but also by expanding its range of services and the types of professionals it employs. In doing so, HOK has established itself as a model modern architectural practice with a scope far beyond that of a traditional firm.

Moving beyond solely providing pure architectural services to its many clients, HOK has, like some of its competitors, entered allied fields, from engineering to interior design. A client can come to HOK for a master plan, the design of a religious building, or technical assistance with the development of scientific laboratories, all executed at the highest level by specialists. Strategic planning is also available to clients who want to rethink the way in which their physical environment impacts the way their organizations function, a professional service that goes well beyond the design of architecture. Global entities can obtain solutions to their built environment requirements, tailored to each of their locations—from locals on the ground who are intimately familiar with their respective region. HOK has the capacity to address myriad client requests, but not by purveying cookie-cutter services. Instead, HOK prides itself on responding with professional rigor and innovative thinking.

Perhaps most interestingly, the firm has also put considerable time and energy into the problem of how best to advance the practice of architecture, not just by adding related services that are already well established, but also by examining what has not yet been done by architects but could be. In doing so, HOK is following a compelling strategy of seeking new opportunities beyond standard practice, what professors W. Chan Kim and Renée Mauborgne have termed a "blue ocean strategy," a metaphor of an open sea, clear of competitors.

It is not that HOK shuns competition nor is it giving up any of its existing activities, but its pursuit of territory in the "blue ocean" signifies its desire to expand the areas in which architects operate and reflects its firm-wide belief in the ongoing metamorphosis of the firm itself. This means that a much wider set of opportunities is available for both the employees of HOK and for their clients. In the past, architecture firms primarily hired architects. Today, HOK employs a host of professionals from outside the architectural profession, including business strategists akin to management consultants. One practice in particular, the Advance Strategies Group, functions directly in this fashion. They explore the depths of their clients' organizations and needs in order to interpret how best to fine-tune the clients' working environments. This group often embeds its professionals within the client's location, a close-knit arrangement that enhances HOK's ability to predict what will work best for the client, often in advance of a direct request—a learning experience for both parties.

This is just one example of HOK's innovative outreach to clients and its commitment to transforming the firm into a much broader purveyor of services. Architecture is not just about building; it's a proxy for how people organize themselves and their institutions and therefore is deserving of a central place within an organization's internal strategy. HOK sees its role as a key professional partner with clients in their efforts to improve their built environment and therefore their ability to work, to present themselves to a wider public, and to plan for their future needs. In this way, HOK is far more than a designer providing beautiful settings, which of course it still does. It is also an essential participant in the ongoing success of its clients, from employing cutting-edge technology for the District of Columbia Consolidated Forensic Laboratory to developing innovative responses to the problem of how best to deliver cardiovascular care in hospital facilities. The widest range of projects and problems crosses the desks of HOK, which drives the firm's active engagement in research throughout a host of topics.

There are several elements that define HOK's ethos. Without question, the firm is dedicated to producing high-quality structures that enhance the environment. But the firm has more on its agenda than simply creating good-looking products.

First, HOK's people begin with what they term "thought leadership," the introduction of key ideas that will drive a project and add to the client's understanding of what is truly possible given the variety of constraints any project confronts. Second, HOK is strongly committed to the goal of sustainability—of using resources as wisely as possible and acting in a way that provides stewardship of natural settings. While sustainability has become a key catchphrase for many well-meaning institutions, HOK has put this commitment into action by implementing concrete strategies which have allowed it to produce designs that intelligently utilize energy and other resources with a keen eye to the future. The firm has published a major text on the subject, *The HOK Guidebook to Sustainable Design*, now in its second edition, underscoring its leadership on this increasingly important subject.

A related aspect of the HOK professional outlook has to do with its commitment to cities, embodied in so much of its work. From master plans to the design and refurbishment of public space in major urban areas, HOK has made its dedication to the importance of cities an integral aspect of its practice. The firm's professionals believe strongly in producing designs that add significantly to the urban experience and that will be welcomed by visitors and residents alike. Part of that challenge comes from understanding the cities themselves and the cultures that support them. This goes back to HOK's extensive network of offices, which makes most jobs brought to HOK local in nature.

HOK performs extensive research into how the specifics of place will affect each project and it is this research that drives the design process.

It is often hard to imagine how any firm can grow to the size that HOK has, especially one with such global reach. HOK's structure mirrors that of many of its clients who have become global players and therefore may not just be an unusual development but an essential one for the future. HOK has kept up with its corporate clients as they have expanded into the many corners of the world. The advantages are significant, making HOK one of the few firms that can handle massively scaled projects, from full campuses, such as the 6.5-million-square-foot KAUST (King Abdullah University of Science and Technology in Saudi Arabia) to transportation hubs like Amsterdam's Passenger Terminal.

With KAUST, the firm put multiple offices to work on the project in order to "race the sun" (work around the clock) to produce the elaborate and scientifically advanced design under an extremely tight schedule. Very few firms are set up to handle this type of demanding schedule, but HOK is. HOK's many offices have an additional advantage: the firm today employs a dynamic system that connects all of its professionals. While specific expertise may be developed in one location or the other, all offices have the ability to tap into that wealth of talent when required. Widespread collaboration is encouraged.

Overall, the firm has a dedication to social consciousness, which encompasses its belief in sustainability and commitment to cities. That social consciousness is applied to the way in which buildings act as good neighbors in their respective communities, the manner that communities and cities can be made more livable for their residents, and also in the way the firm treats its own people. HOK wants to provide extraordinary results for its clients, but it also wants to have a respectful, collegial, invigorating environment for all of its employees. That attitude makes its way into firm-wide policies that ensure that the individuals who constitute a larger HOK are cultivated professionally and encouraged to advance within their specific specialties.

In a world where many design firms were founded on the ideas of a single individual, this is a particularly refreshing path to follow. Positive support for individual accomplishment and growth within the firm's structure, where new ideas are actively encouraged and collaboration among colleagues is reinforced, should certainly yield interesting, intelligent results, not to mention more satisfied practitioners. The ultimate goal, of course, is to produce the best design, writ large, for the greater community. As the pages that follow attest, that is now being accomplished. Now in its second half-century in architecture, HOK appears to be on that trajectory for decades to come.

Hilary Lewis

Selected Projects

40 Peak Road Residential Development

Hong Kong, China

20,720 square feet / 1,925 square meters
Completion: 2004

1

1   House E stairway

2   Site plan

3   Balcony view

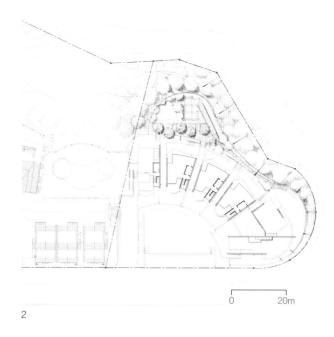

0   20m

2

Situated at the crest of The Peak, this five-home development is on a site offering a panoramic view to the north to Wanchai and across the harbor to Tsimshatsui. The views to the south look down over rolling hills to the south coast of Hong Kong island and Aberdeen.

3

5

The five single-family homes average 4,145 square feet (385 square meters). In response to site conditions and to emphasize the individuality of the houses, three separate house types are provided within the development.

House A, the courtyard house, is a bookend defining the site's western edge. The house is longer and narrower than its neighbors, with light flooding into the center of the house through a semi-enclosed courtyard. House B (of which there are three) eliminates corridors in favor of a large circulation hub. The geometry of this house creates, and is a product of, the fan-shaped site layout. The geometry of House C reconciles the termination of the plan with the linear edge of Peak Road.

4　View from swimming pool

5　Night view

4

150 California

San Francisco, California, USA

205,000 square feet / 19,000 square meters
Completion: 1999

1   Façade detail

2   View of office tower

Providing unity to a building that straddles two districts was the design goal for this 23-story office tower. Anchoring the corner of Front and California Streets, the building is in the heart of San Francisco's financial district and, as part of the Front–California conservation district, was subject to a historic preservation ordinance.

The design and materials provide architectural unity between the two districts while accommodating the complex massing requirements. The building exterior includes a limestone base with a granite curtain wall and a 330-foot-high (101-meter) steel and glass tower. The sense of scale and richness of detail complement the urban fabric.

1

2

3

3   Pedestrian plaza

4   Lobby

5   Building transition

6   Site plan

7   Glass mechanical penthouse

4

5

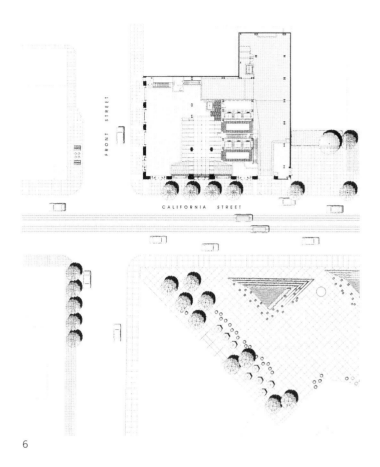

6

The California Street elevation is punctuated by a bow-front steel and glass window bay that marks the entrance and extends vertically to a glass mechanical penthouse. A glass bar along the west façade acknowledges the transition between districts and accentuates the dramatic verticality. Inside, the flexible floor plates range from approximately 6,000 to 14,000 rentable square feet (557 to 1,300 square meters).

7

1

Accenture Offices

Seattle, Washington, USA

50,000 square feet / 4,645 square meters
Completion: 2000

1   Reception area

2   Open, public work area

3   Private work space

3

2

Building the design concept around the four elements—water, air, earth, and fire—creates a framework for satisfying Accenture's workplace and image goals.

Space for professional staff is not specifically dedicated, giving it a hospitality feel. Services offered are reminiscent of those found at a five-star hotel, with a "concierge" assigning space based on the staff member's need for private or collaborative environments. Touchdown stations, office rooms, breakout areas, and conference spaces support a range of activities.

The plan creates four major neighborhoods, each consisting of open and enclosed workspaces, collaboration rooms, informal open spaces, and ancillary storage, printer, copy, and pantry areas.

The design distinguishes neighborhoods by introducing characteristics of the four elements in the forms, furnishings, light fixtures, colors, artwork, and materials. Colored glass, maple wood, and light-colored fabrics lend the dense plan an open, airy feeling. Use of accent furniture and decorative lamps augments the soft, warm atmosphere.

4   Hallway view

5   Informal meeting space

4

AGL Resources Headquarters Renovation

Atlanta, Georgia, USA

225,000 square feet / 20,900 square meters
Completion: 2003

1   "Neighborhood" community center

2   Main reception lobby

AGL gutted and completely renovated an iconic Atlanta office tower to create a new high-performance work environment with a contemporary Southern image. The new office space supports the company's traditional values while demonstrating AGL's position as a community leader.

The organizing concept for a typical floor is based on different "neighborhoods"—business units, departments, or teams—grouped together with their managers. Each neighborhood includes offices, workstations, a variety of different team areas, support and break space, touchdown/visitor spaces, and a central community center.

The universal plan allocates space based on generic space types, which can be easily reconfigured without the considerable costs associated with customized build-outs. The use of common design elements, finishes and artwork on public spaces, typical floors, and executive spaces helps visually link the areas and promotes a sense of community.

1

Alfred A. Arraj United States Courthouse

Denver, Colorado, USA

318,550 square feet / 29,600 square meters
Completion: 2002
Architect of record: Anderson Mason Dale P.C.

1   Entrance

2   Overall view

The courthouse tower and low pavilion are proportionally balanced in response to the surrounding Federal District and urban context and are in keeping with the city's architectural heritage. The tower is composed of a series of vertically oriented rectangular planes; above the open framework at the top is a floating horizontal roof incorporating photovoltaic panels.

2

3

4

3 Rotunda stair

4 Sundial

5 Entry detail

The two-story pavilion, an arrangement of geometric forms under a larger horizontal roof, acts as the frontispiece to the entire complex while recalling the traditional town-square courthouse.

In addition to the photovoltaic system, other energy-efficient measures include extensive daylighting and underfloor displacement ventilation. These measures are projected to reduce energy consumption by 40 percent compared to a conventional design. Building materials were carefully selected to embody sustainable design principles.

Allsteel Resource Center Showroom and Offices

Atlanta, Georgia, USA

13,000 square feet / 1,210 square meters
Completion: 2006

Boston, Massachusetts, USA

12,400 square feet / 1,150 square meters
Completion: 2006

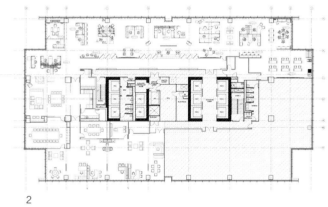

2

1   Reception
2   Floor plan

This LEED-CI Gold certified design expresses the energy, materials, and colors indigenous to the Southeast.

A community room acts as the heart of the space and creates a southern lodge experience while offering city views. The wood-slat ceiling resembles a barn structure, while the limestone fireplace gives the feeling of an old chimney in an open field. A long hallway connecting the reception area to the community room provides the experience of driving down a long country road.

The open-plan office area doubles as a showroom where Allsteel can highlight its workplace solutions.

3

4

This LEED-CI certified resource center/showroom takes its cues from the surrounding historic Boston architecture. Located in the city's Faneuil Hall Marketplace district, the showroom overlooks Boston Harbor and is adjacent to the famous Quincy Market.

The design of the showroom is understated in order to enhance the workspace solutions on display. Stone reminiscent of Boston's cobblestone streets lines the floors, limestone is used for wall surfaces, and the entrance floor features Vermont slate. Other materials, including cherry wood veneer panels, painted glass panels, and steel reflect the visible layers of Boston's architecture.

The centerpiece community room is a casual conversation space featuring a cozy fireplace and comfortable seating. A large counter-height meeting table features a glass top etched with an antique map depicting Boston Harbor.

3   Showroom
4   Workplace showroom

America Online
Regional Headquarters

Beverly Hills, California, USA

65,000 square feet / 6,040 square meters
Completion: 2006

1   Internet café

2   Rotunda

America Online's regional headquarters in Beverly Hills
consolidates AOL's Los Angeles-area business units into
a single location that provides flexibility for growth.
In addition to offices, hoteling zones, and meeting rooms,
the headquarters includes a broadcast studio that takes
up almost half the ground level along with support spaces
including an audiovisual room and two green rooms.

The design brands the space, originally designed as the
home of DreamWorks SKG, as AOL's.

2

A street-level Internet café provides a comfortable spot where employees can access the Internet with their laptops while relaxing and socializing. Frosted and clear glass panels open the café to the public.

Translucent glass walls in "heads-down" office areas convey a feeling of camaraderie and privacy. Rounded corners dissipate the regimented feel of the right angle, which can be psychologically constricting.

3

3 Third-floor office area

4 Executive secretary and directors' offices

4

Amsterdam Passenger Terminal

Amsterdam, The Netherlands

280,000 square feet / 26,000 square meters
Completion: 2000

1   Viewing platform

2   Interior view

The Passenger Terminal Amsterdam is located on the
south bank of the River IJ, a modern urban environment
close to the old city center. With its striking undulating
roof, the Passenger Terminal is a memorable first glimpse
of Amsterdam for arriving cruise ship passengers. The
building has a 1,970-foot-long (600-meter) quay, large
reception halls, convention, and parking facilities.

2

3

The transparent nature of the building allows passengers and visitors constant visual contact with arriving and departing cruise ships. Two great arcs of glass—60 feet (18 meters) high on the waterside and 80 feet (24 meters) high on the landside—provide dramatic views of ships for embarking passengers and frame views of the historic inner harbor and city skyline for disembarking passengers.

Cobalt blue tiling on all vertical circulation assists wayfinding while heavy timber beams recall Amsterdam's shipbuilding tradition.

3   Entrance and carport
4   Interior view looking east

4

Anaheim Convention Center

Anaheim, California, USA

850,000 square feet / 79,000 square meters
Completion: 2001

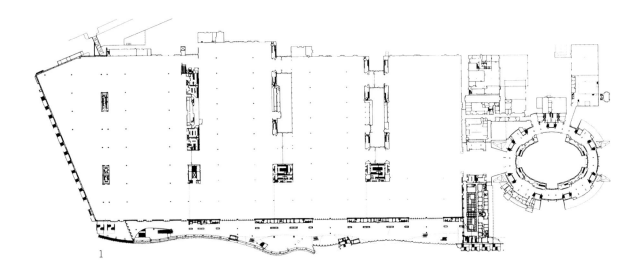

1

The Anaheim Convention Center is the largest convention center on the West Coast, accommodating approximately one million convention attendees annually. This expansion, which consolidated the center into a more efficient and attractive venue, added exhibit halls, meeting rooms, a ballroom, and prefunction space.

A new entrance announces the facility's updated image and conveys its role as an important civic structure. Because the Center was on a very tight site, expansion had to be vertical.

1   Floor plan

2   Light-filled circulation space

2

3

The ground floor was extended out in a curvilinear form along the building's length as far as possible for new registration and additional exhibit hall space. Meeting rooms and ballroom—with accompanying delegate circulation and service circulation forming a unique interlocking layout—were then constructed over this new "found" space on two upper levels. To accomplish this, the street between the Hilton Hotel and the Center was removed and a garden was created.

Approaching the central rotunda along the axial entry drive recalls Spanish Missions, Grumman's Theater, or the Disneyland Fantasyland Castle. The design reflects a Southern California "spirit of place." Forms, colors, and materials are rooted in the land, architecture, and culture found in and around Anaheim.

3   Circulation space from above

4   Façade detail

4

Barclays Bank Headquarters

London, UK

670,000 square feet / 62,245 square meters
Completion: 2004

1 Barclays Tower in Canary Wharf context

2 West elevation

3 Cladding detail

1

The design of this 513-foot (156-meter) tower at London's Canary Wharf creates large, adaptable work environments and provides flexibility for tenants to grow or sublet space.

A series of six-story, south-facing atria offer places for recreation, relaxation, and informal work while maximizing

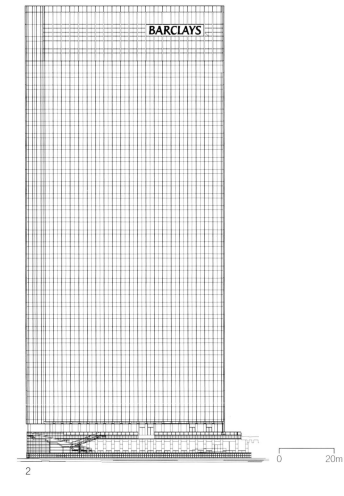

2

4

natural light and views. The steel and glass façade was designed to catch the northern European sun, reflect the color of the sky, and complement the neighboring buildings on the Canary Wharf Estate. Stainless steel shadow box spandrels suggest a pristine jewel-box effect.

The U-shaped floor plate creates a visual connection among occupants and encourages collaboration.

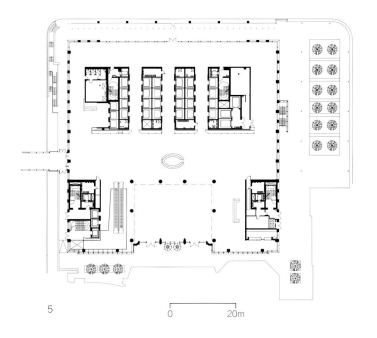

5

0   20m

6

4   View from Canada Place

5   Ground floor plan

6   Vertical view from entrance

7

Amenities include a health and fitness center, a 365-seat restaurant, and training facilities. The ground-floor lobby, one of the largest in Canary Wharf, provides a setting for major artwork.

The building, located at 1 Churchill Place, provides covered access to the Jubilee Line, Docklands Light Railway Stations, and the major retail facilities of Canary Wharf. Twenty-one floors are devoted to the headquarters of Barclays Bank.

7   Main entrance lobby

8   View from office with atrium to right

1

Barnes-Jewish Hospital
Center for Advanced Medicine

St. Louis, Missouri, USA

1 million square feet / 93,000 square meters
Completion: 2001

2

1 Glass feature

2 Tower sky view

3 Site plan

3

The Center for Advanced Medicine is part of a world-class medical campus that integrates Barnes Hospital, Jewish Hospital, and Children's Hospital with the Washington University School of Medicine complex. The 14-story, glass-clad tower acts as the gateway to the medical center. It houses a state-of-the-art facility that provides specialist outpatient services to almost 3,000 patients daily.

4

The design reflects a "patients first" philosophy in the provision of outpatient medical services. The entire patient experience, from access and parking, to wayfinding, waiting, treatment, recovery, and social areas, was carefully examined to provide a seamless, emotionally supportive environment not only for patients, but also for family members, staff, and physicians. The design includes a light-filled atrium, which is a major interior organizational element, and large open flexible floor plans with plenty of natural light. Bright, comfortable common areas finished in warm neutral tones contribute to the calm, healing environment.

4   Reception with atrium

5   Atrium

Barranca del Muerto 329

Mexico City, Mexico

220,000 square feet / 20,438 square meters
Completion: 2003

1   Barranca del Muerto Avenue pedestrian view

2   Main entrance

The goal for this project was to create Triple-A-class office space inside an efficient building envelope without sacrificing design. The design sets a rectangular floor plate onto an irregular site, creating a grand triangular entrance plaza that nestles into the surrounding urban fabric.

To maximize the built area, the floor plates were extended to the eastern and western edges of the site, where two massive concrete walls define the building limits. Between these walls, a series of simple glass panes stretch from one end to the other. Aluminum shading devices and varying mullion depths create an exciting composition of light, shade, and shadow on the main building façade.

2

Biogen Idec Campus

San Diego, California, USA

350,000 square feet / 32,500 square meters
Completion: 2004

1   Model

2   Lobby

The plan works with the existing terrain to develop a central arroyo space reminiscent of an original natural feature of the chaparral site. Arranging the connected office buildings and labs on either side of the central open space takes advantage of the land by "stepping down" into the arroyo. Public entrances to the buildings are oriented toward external gardens and perimeter parking at the higher elevations, while employees access the arroyo at a lower level along the internal edge. The two sides of the campus are joined by a pedestrian bridge that spans the arroyo and ties the main entrance lobby with the commons building.

These office and research environments are completely different from the cold, stark interiors that characterize the facilities of many biotech companies.

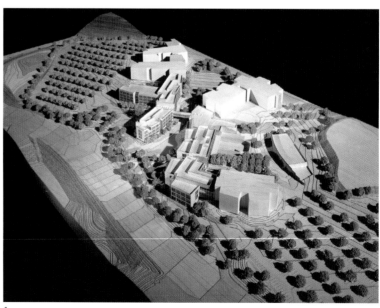

1

2

3   Site plan

4   Café

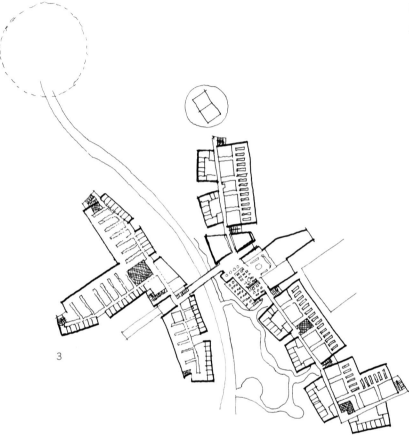

3

The richly textured natural finishes, abundant natural light, and
warm color palette all support Biogen Idec's concern for its
patients and staff.

Cleft limestone wall cladding, variegated teak flooring, and cherry
lattice paneling convey natural warmth, scale, and texture.
A hospitable, residential quality prevails in the reception and
executive areas. Displays featuring patients, caregivers, and
employees are scattered throughout the building to illustrate core
values. There is a feeling of understated elegance and human
interest throughout the site.

6

Amenities include an espresso bar, cafeteria, fitness
center, and three-story reception area. The bridge joining
the administrative buildings and laboratory buildings
offers panoramic campus views and seating areas.

5   Arroyo

6   Terraced conferencing area

Bladensburg High School

Bladensburg, Maryland, USA

304,562 square feet / 28,295 square meters

Completion: 2004

Joint venture partner: WMCRP Architects

1

1   Entrance detail

2   Night view of entry

The 19-acre, steep-sloped site was a deviation from the typical secondary school site, which is 40 acres of extremely flat land. The designers responded to the challenge by giving the building a prominent presence in its surroundings and creatively using the natural resources to complement the school's image.

Though the building program was typical for a high school in Prince George's County, the image of Bladensburg is atypical. Unlike other schools in the area, the program areas were designed to incorporate some sculptural features and a less conventional atmosphere.

A five-story academic wing is linked to other areas in an L-shape massing that embraces the stadium playing field.

2

3

4

In addition to having a presence in its surroundings, the building seamlessly blends the academic program with the school's vocational/technical program. The new school, which accommodates more than 1,900 students, includes an auditorium, a technical academy, and a wellness center.

The gym roof is lined with photovoltaic panels that reduce the school's energy use. Other green features include aerated concrete, masonry units, and operable windows.

3   Building arcade

4   Academic building and athletic field

1

Boeing Leadership Center Campus and Carriage House

St. Louis, Missouri, USA

8,570 square feet / 800 square meters
Completion: 1999

1   Leadership Center arrival

2   Aerial view

The desire to create a collaborative learning environment that provides a place for people to come together to exchange information and redesign processes—to learn to think differently—drove the design of Boeing's new Leadership Center. The Center includes residential lodges with 204 private rooms, a workshop building with six high-tech classrooms, a gourmet dining area, an 80-person theater-style lecture hall, a fitness center, and 21 breakout rooms.

The design creates a contemporary, attractive facility that communicates the message that the company values its employees while housing sophisticated high-tech learning tools.

The 286-acre rural site rests on bluffs overlooking the confluence of two rivers in St. Louis County. The campus

2

includes 5 miles of paved trails, a softball field carved into the woods, and active farmland.

The renovation of Boeing's Leadership Center incorporates three historic buildings, including a circa-1952, 8,570-square-foot (800-square-meter) Carriage House. The two-story Carriage House is a limestone-clad building with a mezzanine level suspended from the building's glue-laminated beam structural system. Breakout areas are located in the mezzanine, which is defined by the mansard roof.

The renovated Carriage House serves as a learning laboratory for Boeing's leaders. Ordinary materials are simply detailed in a natural palette influenced by the existing architecture and the estate's rural history. Furnishings and equipment were selected for their mobility and adaptability.

3   Carriage House entrance

4   Carriage House mezzanine level teaming space

5   Carriage House breakout area

5

Capital One Canada Offices

North York, Ontario, Canada

22,000 square feet / 2,045 square meters
Completion: 2005

1

Capital One Canada wished to establish a unique new identity in Canada while expanding its office space. Its aim was also to attract the best and brightest MBA graduates and elite financial services professionals to the company.

The employee-focused design includes bright, open spaces, filled with natural light. In a radical departure from its American division, Capital One Canada implemented a workplace concept in which all staff—including managers—have a dedicated space with a 30 x 72-inch desk, storage tower, and small mobile side table. Wireless technology enables employees to move freely from their desks to meeting rooms or the staff lounge.

1 Staff area

2 Work pods color

2

1

Central Japan International Airport (Chubu Centrair) Terminal

Tokoname City, Aichi, Japan

2.36 million square feet / 219,250 square meters
Completion: 2005

1   Drop-off canopy

2   Departure level plan

3   Landside view

This airport is located on a manmade island off the coast of Tokoname, a suburb of Nagoya.

Patterned after the Japanese art of origami, the airport's T shape reflects its aeronautical function. The roof structure and architecture are composed of a series of folded glass and metal planes accented by natural light. Light fabric is used on skylight elements.

Interior gardens integrate the landscape into the architecture, serving as pleasant green areas with plenty of natural light as well as wayfinding elements. The wall and floor materials are from a light warm palette, keeping the environment warm and inviting all year. Lighting throughout the departure hall and main concourse is indirect, increasing the drama of the main roof structure. A large upper-level concession area adjacent to the main departure hall provides access to an event space and exterior observation areas under a dramatic glassed sloping roof.

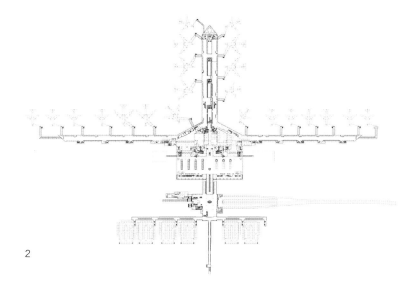

2

3

4

Planned and designed by a joint venture of HOK, Nikken Sekkei, Azusa Sekkei, and Ove Arup, the passenger terminal complex includes a main terminal building, two linear concourses, and a central pier for a total of 13 international and nine domestic gates, with an additional 14 hardstand positions.

4   Central garden

5   Concession mezzanine

5

Chevy Chase Center

Chevy Chase, Maryland, USA

412,000 square feet / 38,275 square meters
Completion: 2006

1   Retail buildings

2   Detail of retail buildings

1

This project involved the redevelopment of offices, restaurants, and retail stores in one of the country's most successful neighborhood shopping centers. High-end boutique retailers are the main attraction.

The project, which quadrupled the size of the Center, included the design of a two-story retail building, a three-story office and retail building, an eight-story office building, and a two-story neighborhood retail center.

The Center is directly adjacent to the Chevy Chase/ Friendship Heights Metro station. The project promotes pedestrian activity near this station by creating a central retail area that supports business growth and evening

3

social activities. Two public parks and a wide streetscape with specialty lighting and high-quality street furnishings add appeal for pedestrians. Adjacent buildings and a large wall of water surrounded by trees and flowers create an enclosed feeling and help define the space.

3   Fountain

4   Office building

4

Children's Discovery Museum

San Jose, California, USA

7,200 square feet / 670 square meters
Completion: 2004

1   View toward main stage from courtyard

2   View through arcade window

1

The design of the amphitheater renovation as an "outdoor learning laboratory" provides children with a stimulating, hands-on environment for creative play and a museum with a flexible outdoor space. The design complements the unique expression of the building's original architecture while creating a contemporary adaptation of a traditional Mexican courtyard. The design features an open plan, color, texture, and robust succulent planting.

Within the courtyard are two performance stages: a small stage at the lower courtyard level and an enhanced large performance stage at the upper museum level. The large stage is shaded by a structure of horizontal aluminum louvers that provide filtered shade throughout the day

2

3

4

5

3   Water tunnel detail

4   View from southwest

5   View through west entry

without impeding visibility at night or during performances. A curved wall finished in handmade Mexican tile serves as the backdrop for the small performance stage. A serpentine planter wall along the north end of the courtyard is cast in concrete and designed with a series of levels incorporating seating, a water "runnel," and drought-tolerant planting. The plant palette, a mix of ornamental grasses, succulent groundcover, and cacti, is highly sculptural against the backdrop of purple stucco.

This multi-use outdoor space serves as a venue for a wide array of functions, including music/theatrical/dance performances, fund-raising galas, community events, and after-school and summer programs.

Cisco Systems Executive Briefing Center

San Jose, California, USA

40,000 square feet / 3,715 square meters
Completion: 2005

1 Emerging technology area

2 Lighting detail

2

Cisco's new Executive Briefing Center at the company's headquarters in San Jose is used as a high-tech conference center for showcasing products and services to Fortune 150 business leaders and international dignitaries.

The design of the center highlights Cisco's technology and delivers powerful sales messages to potential customers. A glass-enclosed demonstration area promotes user interaction by providing computer stations on pedestals and showcasing a room full of actual hardware.

3

4

Changeable screens and panels communicate Cisco's brand while interacting with guests.

Materials are high-quality without being ostentatious or expensive. Sustainable materials include rapidly renewable bamboo flooring that adds warmth to the neutral color scheme. An array of color-changing LED lighting is embedded into the ceilings above the touchdown lounges, which are placed outside conference rooms and feature comfortable couches and carpet.

3   Touchdown area

4   Touchdown view to demonstration area

5   Customer testimonial area

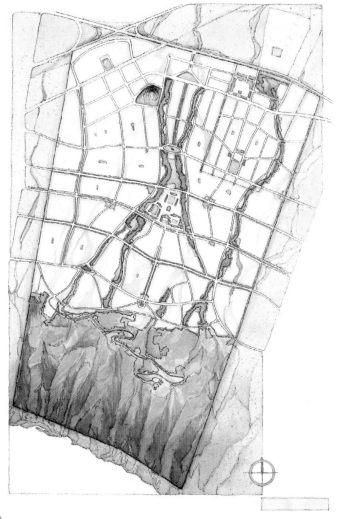

The master plan for Ciudad Mitras envisions a beautiful and sustainable series of communities designed using the tenets of great urbanism—with full services and many options for living, working, shopping, worshipping, and socializing—all within the boundaries of a 4,450-acre (1,800-hectare) site in northern Mexico.

The Ciudad Mitras plan responds to the rich natural features of a mountain site and the heritage of its neighboring cities.

Ciudad Mitras Master Plan

Monterrey, Mexico

4,450 acres / 1,800 hectares
Completion: 2004

1   Northwest view from town square

2   Illustrative master plan

3   View south from entry

3

Set upon undeveloped agricultural land along a westward advancing growth corridor at the base of the Las Mitras mountain range, Ciudad Mitras will combine traditional settlement patterns of Nuevo León, a strong architectural identity, and a wealth of sustainable development practices.

The master plan features a combination of compact development and respect and celebration of its numerous arroyos, or water-carved channels; a complete range of building types; a hierarchical network of streets, trails and pathways; functional and beautiful public and open spaces; and educational, civic, and cultural program elements—all based on the traditions of the Mexican barrio or neighborhood system.

This development will provide opportunities for mass transit connections and roadway extensions from this expanding area, linking Ciudad Mitras to the cities of Monterrey and Garcia.

Community Hospital of the Monterey Peninsula

Monterey, California, USA

270,000 square feet / 25,100 square meters
Completion: 2006

1 Aerial view

2 Healing garden corner detail

This expansion to a community hospital doubled the hospital's size while providing it with the best technology based on the most modern care protocols. The project includes two new patient care pavilions, incorporating state-of-the-art operating suites and 120 new patient rooms; a parking garage; and renovations to existing buildings.

The design supports the hospital's emphasis on delivering the highest-quality care with a human touch that fosters healing. Low, striking rooflines, sweeping views to the Pacific Ocean and Monterey Pine forests, and naturally lit public spaces contribute to the calm, healing environment. The new architecture matches the original buildings designed by Edward Durrell Stone, allowing old and new buildings to merge as one.

1

2

Community of Christ World Headquarters

Independence, Missouri, USA

130,000 square feet / 12,100 square meters
Competion: 1993

1

2

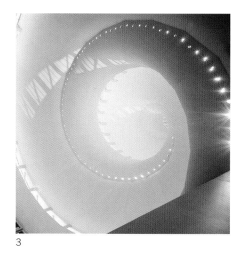

3

The design of this temple and worship headquarters was inspired by the intricate spiral of the nautilus seashell, a form governed by the same natural laws that shape the human umbilical cord, rams' horns, and nebulas found in space. As a symbol of nature found all over the world in many different cultures, the spiral is a fitting symbol of the church's global presence.

The 200-foot base creates a sense of intimacy by seating more than 1,600 people in a circular arrangement. From the base, the temple tapers skyward from a stainless-steel spire that peaks at 300 feet. The whirls broaden in a geometric progression, each revolution of the spiral generating an upward and uplifting focus.

1   Nautilus seashell inspiration

2   Aerial view of spire

3   Interior of spire

4   Entrance to main sanctuary

4

Confluence Greenway and Great Rivers Greenway Master Plan

St. Louis, Missouri, USA

1,400 square miles / 3,625 square kilometers
Completion: 2000

1   Regional context

2   Confluence of Missouri and Mississippi Rivers

Since the mid-1990s, a greenway movement in metropolitan St. Louis has included a Gateway Parks and Trails initiative to establish a regional bi-state park district.

Concurrent with the initiative was the completion of the Confluence Greenway plan, which creates a massive, perpetually sustainable 40-mile riverside park that encompasses 200 square miles of natural, agricultural, and developed land. The plan extends from the Gateway Arch in downtown St. Louis to the Mississippi River's confluences with the Missouri and Illinois Rivers. Linear parks, pedestrian and bicycle trails, conservation areas, and interpretive centers will provide a variety of recreational and educational experiences.

The Confluence Greenway project celebrates the meeting of the Great Rivers as the symbolic, physical, and

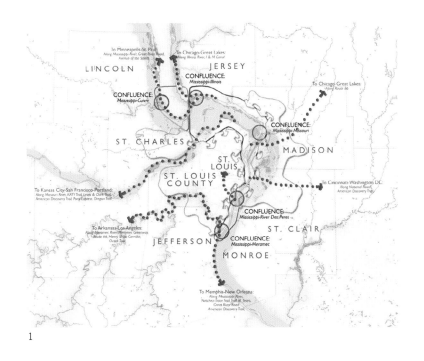

1

2

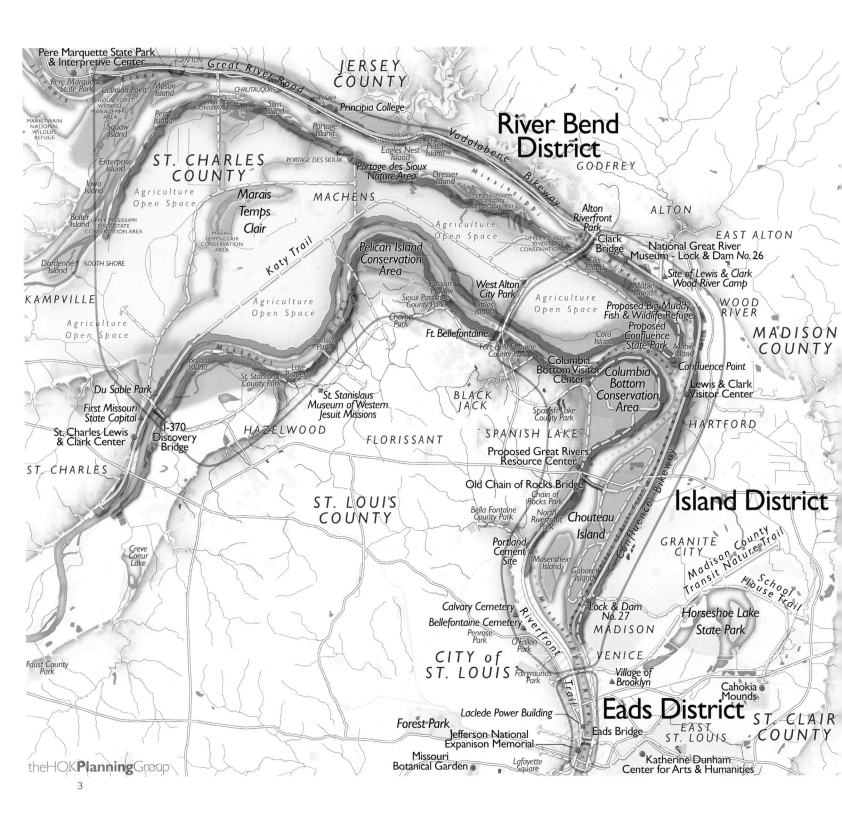

Pere Marquette State Park
& Interpretive Center

GRAFTON

Great River Road

JERSEY
COUNTY

Pere Marquette
State Park

Calhoun Point

CHAUTAUQUA

Mason
Island

CALHOUN POINT
WILDLIFE
MANAGEMENT
AREA

Squaw Island

Perry
Island

UPPER MISSISSIPPI
RIVER STATE
CONSERVATION AREA

ELSAH

Slim
Island

Principia College

Portage
Island

**River Bend
District**

MARK TWAIN
NATIONAL
WILDLIFE
REFUGE

Enterprise
Island

Vadalabene Bikeway

GODFREY

Iowa
Island

ST. CHARLES
COUNTY

PORTAGE DES SIOUX

MARK TWAIN
NATIONAL WILDLIFE REFUGE

Eagles Nest
Island

Piasa
Island

Mississippi

ALTON

Bolter
Island

UPPER MISSISSIPPI
RIVER STATE
CONSERVATION AREA

*Agriculture
Open Space*

Portage des Sioux
Nature Area

Dresser
Island

UPPER MISSISSIPPI
RIVER STATE
CONSERVATION AREA

Alton
Riverfront
Park

EAST ALTON

Dardenne
Island

SOUTH SHORE

MARAIS
TEMPS
CLAIR
CONSERVATION
AREA

MACHENS

*Agriculture
Open Space*

UPPER MISSISSIPPI
RIVER STATE
CONSERVATION AREA

Clark
Bridge

National Great River
Museum - Lock & Dam No. 26

*Marais
Temps
Clair*

Katy Trail

Pelican Island
Conservation
Area

Ellis
Island

Site of Lewis & Clark
Wood River Camp

KAMPVILLE

Possum
Hollow

Sioux Passage
County Park

West Alton
City Park

Maple
Island

*Agriculture
Open Space*

Proposed Big Muddy
Fish & Wildlife Refuge

WOOD
RIVER

*Agriculture
Open Space*

Littles
Island

Proposed
Confluence
State Park

MADISON
COUNTY

*Agriculture
Open Space*

Champ
Park

Ft. Bellefontaine

Cora
Island

Confluence Point

Sunset
Park

Bryan
Island

Love
Property

Missouri

Fort Bellefontaine
County Park

Columbia
Bottom Visitor
Center

Mobile
Island

Lewis & Clark
Visitor Center

Du Sable Park

St. Stanislaus
County Park

St. Stanislaus
Museum of Western
Jesuit Missions

BLACK
JACK

Columbia
Bottom
Conservation
Area

HARTFORD

First Missouri
State Capital

I-370
Discovery
Bridge

Spanish Lake
County Park

St. Charles Lewis
& Clark Center

HAZELWOOD

FLORISSANT

SPANISH LAKE

ST. CHARLES

Proposed Great Rivers
Resource Center

ST. LOUIS
COUNTY

Confluence Bikeway

Island District

Old Chain of Rocks Bridge

Chain of
Rocks Park

Creve
Coeur
Lake

Bella Fontaine
County Park

North
Riverfront
Park

Chouteau
Island

GRANITE
CITY

Madison County
Transit Nature Trail

*School
House Trail*

Portland
Cement
Site

Mosenthein
Island

Gabaret
Island

Faust County
Park

Calvary Cemetery

Bellefontaine Cemetery

Penrose
Park

O'Fallon
Park

Riverfront Trail

Lock & Dam
No. 27

MADISON

Horseshoe Lake
State Park

CITY of
ST. LOUIS

Fairgrounds
Park

VENICE

Village of
Brooklyn

Cahokia
Mounds

Laclede Power Building

Eads District

ST. CLAIR
COUNTY

Forest Park

Jefferson National
Expansion Memorial

Eads Bridge

EAST
ST. LOUIS

Missouri
Botanical Garden

Lafayette
Square

Katherine Dunham
Center for Arts & Humanities

3

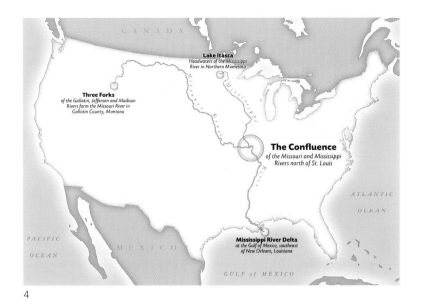

4

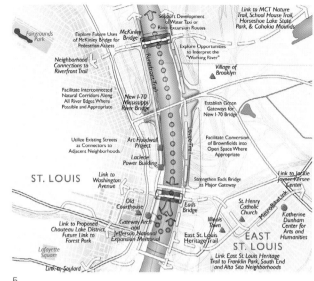

5

6

environmental heart of the St. Louis region. Completion of the greenway will link the region to a growing national green corridor network.

Following public approval of the initiative, HOK designers participated in the Great Rivers Greenway District's citizen-driven visioning plan. This effort defined the "River Ring," an interconnected system of nearly 50 greenways linking three counties, two states, and an area of 1,400 square miles.

3   Master plan

4   National significance

5   Eads district

6   Missouri River

Cork International Airport Passenger Terminal

Cork, Ireland

270,000 square feet / 25,000 square meters
Completion: 2006

1   Departure drop-off curve

2   Skylights over bowstring beams

Following pages:
   Southeast façade

HOK and Jacobs Engineering programmed, planned, and designed the country's first 21st-century airport terminal at Cork International Airport in southern Ireland. The project, which includes a new terminal and multistory parking facility, was built just north of the existing terminal.

The design takes advantage of the sloping site to provide grandstand views of the airfield with a predominantly glass double-height façade. On the landside, the lower building elevation reflects local architecture with stone and rendered walls. The glass, steel, and timber construction maximizes natural daylight. The roof is built of timber and rod bowstring beams on four-limbed tree columns supporting a lightweight steel single-span curved roof deck.

2

4

Capacity at the fast-growing regional airport will increase
from 1.7 million passengers per year to 3 million, with
the ability to further expand the terminal to accommodate
5 million passengers by constructing piers to the north
and south.

4   Departure lounge

5   Head-of-stand road and fixed links

Crystal Tower

Kuwait City, Kuwait

450,000 square feet / 41,800 square meters

Completion: 2009

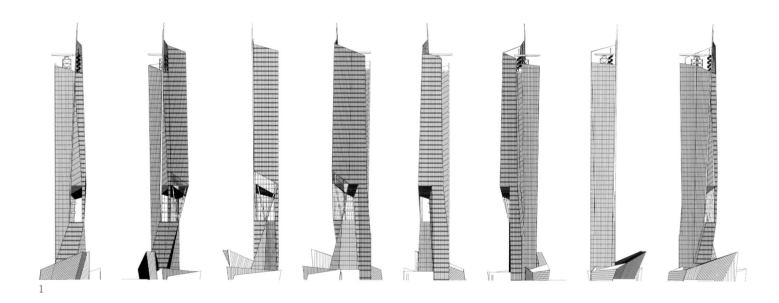

1

This 45-story sister tower to the Intercontinental Hotel and Tower, also designed by HOK, employs a series of angular forms to insert itself into the existing cityscape. The design provides abundant views to the Arabian Gulf and plentiful natural light, refracted through the canted planes of glass. The tower provides a marked, intentional contrast to the sweeping contours of the Intercontinental Hotel and Tower.

1   Building elevation study

2   Exterior rendering

2

3

3   Atrium perspective

4   Bird's-eye view perspective

The Crystal Tower's striking mid-level atrium is open on
three sides and offers a 180-degree vista of downtown
Kuwait City, lending a theatrical presence of negative
space. A precise balancing act recalls the bearings and
proportions of the lower levels in order to reconcile their
horizontal nature with the skyward inclinations of the
overall form.

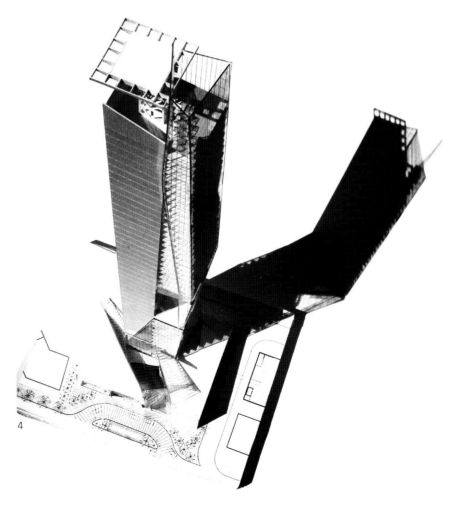

4

Darwin Centre Phase One
at The Natural History Museum

London, UK

120,000 square feet / 11,150 square meters
Completion: 2002

1 Zoomorphic brackets support glass solar wall

2 Solar wall detail

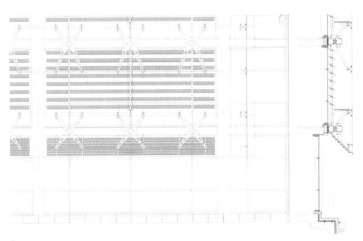

2

This dramatic new glass-clad building is located behind The Natural History Museum, one of London's grandest Romanesque Revival buildings.

Sensitive to its historic setting, the building's contemporary detailing recreates the tradition of "architecture parlante," in which a building's external appearance describes what happens inside. The zoomorphic brackets of the solar wall, the changing appearance created by the sun-tracking metal louvers, and the triple-skin, caterpillar-like inflated roof refer directly to the Darwin Centre's work and mission.

3　Atrium view from top floor

4　West elevation

The louvers in the all-glass solar wall are computer controlled to track the sun, giving the building an "intelligent skin" that changes constantly according to weather conditions and the time of day. The louvers are sandwiched between two layers of glass. As they warm they draw air up from the ground level and out through a linear "chimney" at the top floor, providing a highly efficient cooling mechanism. The lightweight roof requires minimal structural elements for support and the layers of air make it thermally efficient.

The building is composed of three sections: in the front, behind the glass façade, are the offices and laboratories where scientists can be seen at work. At the back is the

4

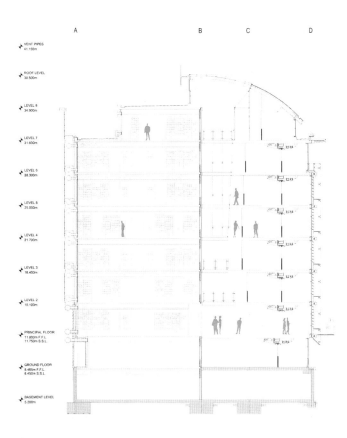

A   B   C   D

VENT PIPES
41.150m

ROOF LEVEL
38.500m

LEVEL 8
34.900m

LEVEL 7
31.600m

LEVEL 6
28.300m

LEVEL 5
25.000m

LEVEL 4
21.700m

LEVEL 3
18.400m

LEVEL 2
15.100m

PRINCIPAL FLOOR
11.800m F.F.L.
11.750m S.S.L.

GROUND FLOOR
8.465m F.F.L
8.450m S.S.L

BASEMENT LEVEL
5.200m

6

seven-story cold store for the specimens. Separating the
two and drawing in natural light is a wedge-shaped atrium
allowing public access to the heart of the building.
Unprecedented behind-the-scenes access to the
museum's collection enables visitors to explore vast
storerooms filled with more than 22 million zoological
specimens while scientists work above them in the privacy
of their labs.

5   Detail view of glass wall

6   Section

1

Dasve Village Master Plan
Lavasa Hill Station
Maharashtra, India

1,800 acres / 750 hectares

1   Aerial view

The master plan proposes transitions from rural areas to the village center so that inhabitants will benefit from not losing touch with traditional ways of life in both rural and urban areas. It is anticipated that the village will grow organically, remaining flexible and culturally appropriate as it evolves.

Geography defines the edges of development of all the villages within the master plan. The Dasve Village town center is located at the confluence of two "nalas," or streams, that converge in the valley floor and empty into a lake, which will provide a recreational amenity and a focal point for the town.

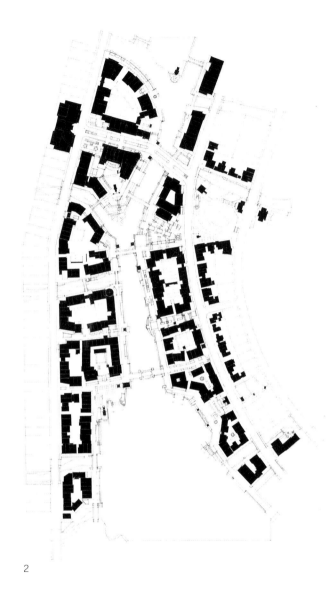

2

3

4

All of the villages within the community will be linked by public transportation that will connect terminals in each village center. Particular attention has been given to pedestrians, to ensure safe navigation in corridors occupied by four- and two-wheeled vehicles, and occasionally animal-drawn carts.

Dasve Village is sustainable in its flexibility. By design, many of the land uses can be interchanged as the market changes.

5

For example, in the town center, the mix of uses may change between ground-floor retail, residential, and potentially even office. In the residential areas, the mix of lot types and unit types can also be modified over time to meet market demand but still respect and enforce urban guidelines. The recreational and tourist attractions can also be modified as corporate and institutional partners become interested in contributing to the development of the hill station.

2   Town center plan

3   Village plan

4   Construction view

5   Town center aerial view

Dechert LLP Law Offices
London, UK

55,000 square feet / 5,110 square meters
Completion: 2005

1   Client meeting room

Dechert's new London law offices and European headquarters are on three floors of "Times Square," a new development on London's Queen Victoria Street.

The design creates a series of neighborhoods grouped around a central three-story atrium that offers views across the floors while promoting interaction. A cellular model of shared offices provides flexibility for future growth.

Two of the three floors contain cellular offices at the perimeter. These offices have glazed fronts that allow natural light into the open-plan space occupied by the administrative staff and allows the lawyers to be seen.

1

2

The third floor contains the reception areas and client-facing conference facilities. Because each space in this compact office environment must be able to help Dechert practice the business of law, the flexible meeting rooms have pivoting and folding walls that allow them to be easily reconfigured.

2   Reception seating area

3   Atrium and break area

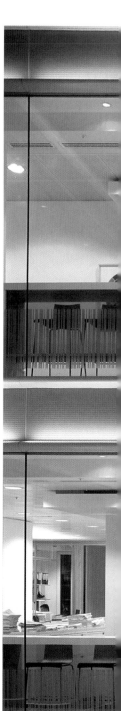

3

1

Dubai Marina Master Plan

Dubai, United Arab Emirates

Master plan: 1,428 acres / 578 hectares

Phase I: 28 acres / 11.5 hectares

Completion: 2005

1   Central fountain

2   Central waterfront plaza

2

Carved along a two-mile stretch of Arabian Gulf shoreline, Dubai Marina is a mixed-use canal-city inspired by the Venetian tradition.

As the world's largest planned waterfront community, the Dubai Marina accommodates 100,000 people in 10 distinct districts. This residential and resort development is shifting the perceived center of Dubai further west along the shore of the Arabian Gulf and advancing the city's transformation into a commercial, entertainment, and resort hub.

3

The first completed phase includes six residential high-rise towers and villas totaling more than 1,000 units connected by a spectacular network of rooftop gardens. In front of the podium structure, a new marina keywall provides an area for a pedestrian and bicycle promenade along a retail colonnade.

Phase 2 will add 2.8 million square feet (260,128 square meters) of mixed-use facilities.

3   Canal edge and waterfront promenade

4   Seating in front of retail arcade

5   Retail arcade along waterfront promenade

4

5

East Taihu Lake Waterfront District

Wujiang, China

1,500 acres / 600 hectares
Completion: 2008

1

1   Waterfront District master plan

2   View of central business district and Taihu Lake waterfront

The vision for the waterfront area and East Taihu Boulevard includes a new urban waterfront community that demonstrates a high level of environmental sustainability and a strong relationship to the water's edge. The underlying framework for this plan provides for the development of an integrated system that utilizes a highly functional grid of interconnected streets, parks, and other public spaces that subsequently creates an open space network connecting various development parcels.

East Taihu Boulevard, a beautifully landscaped urban public space, is intended to host all modes of transportation and is the centerpiece of the master plan for this new waterfront community. With easy access to open space along various waterfront edges, a pedestrian-friendly street network, and a mix of housing types, the East Taihu waterfront development plan will convert long-neglected lakefront into a world-class urban waterfront environment. It will be the center of growth in the Suzhou metropolitan area in the next decade as well as a new attraction close to Shanghai and the Yangtze Delta area.

Edificio Malecon Office Tower

Buenos Aires, Argentina

125,000 square feet / 11,610 square meters
Completion: 1999

1   Main entry

2   Tower detail

1

This 12-story tower was designed as one of Buenos Aires' most technologically advanced office buildings. Constructed on the original basement and foundations of a demolished warehouse, the building features a cast-in-place concrete frame clad with an aluminum and glass curtain wall.

2

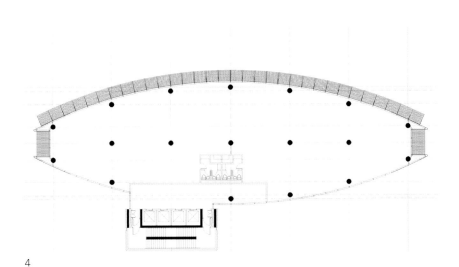

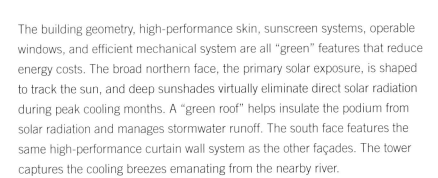

4

5

The building geometry, high-performance skin, sunscreen systems, operable windows, and efficient mechanical system are all "green" features that reduce energy costs. The broad northern face, the primary solar exposure, is shaped to track the sun, and deep sunshades virtually eliminate direct solar radiation during peak cooling months. A "green roof" helps insulate the podium from solar radiation and manages stormwater runoff. The south face features the same high-performance curtain wall system as the other façades. The tower captures the cooling breezes emanating from the nearby river.

Other innovative features include floor plate configuration, building envelope technologies, integration of data and telecommunications, efficient HVAC systems, and improved control technologies.

The building won the prestigious Argentinean Biennale award for the best facility in the nation built over a two-year span. The American Institute of Architects named Edificio Malecon one of the "Top 10 Green Projects" in 2002.

3   Sunscreen system detail

4   Floor plate

5   View of tower

1

Emerson Grand Basin / *Post-Dispatch* Lake in Forest Park

St. Louis, Missouri, USA

76 acres / 31 hectares

Completion: 2003

1   Panoramic view toward Art Hill and St. Louis Art Museum

2   1916 Cass Gilbert plan to enlarge Art Hill and Grand Basin
    (*Saint Louis Art Museum, Museum purchase 1916*)

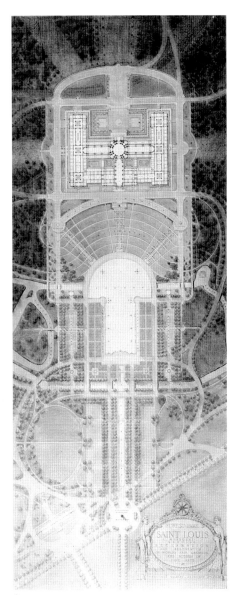

2

The site of the 1904 World's Fair, St. Louis's Forest Park had deteriorated over many decades of deferred maintenance. This master plan was initiated by a renewed emphasis on the historic prominence and grandeur of the Park, including its central gathering place, the Grand Basin, and other features including Art Hill and *Post-Dispatch* Lake. All have been restored to their former glory as part of the rehabilitation program.

3

4

The Grand Basin is a public gathering place with dramatic fountains, benches, formal pathways, and trails to entice park users. The connection between the Grand Basin and Art Hill creates a natural amphitheater for community and special events. The view from atop Art Hill is a seductive urban panorama in what is now one of the finest urban parks in the country.

The project required close collaboration with a number of other professionals, including other designers, an arborist, and civil, structural, hydrology, and geotechnical engineers.

3   Restored suspension bridge over lagoon

4   Grand Basin fountains

5   Reconstructed containment wall

6   Pedestrian bridge connecting Art Hill to Grand Basin

138

5

6

Federal Reserve Bank of Cleveland Headquarters Expansion and Renovation

Cleveland, Ohio, USA

700,000 square feet / 65,000 square meters
Completion: 1998

1   Façade detail

2   Elevation

3   New annex

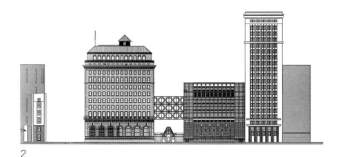

2

The design for the renovation of this historically significant building in downtown Cleveland incorporates high-quality, complementary materials, scale, setbacks, and forms to establish a compatible relationship between the existing building and a new 270,000-square-foot (25,083-square-meter) annex.

3

141

4

To supply the same marble for the new building as on the existing structure, a dormant quarry in Georgia was re-opened and a new technique of attaching the marble to the building was invented. Slots, cantilevers, inserts, folds, spheres, and brackets are positioned and sized within the marble façade in ways that would not have been possible in traditional construction. Thus, traditional details are abstracted to create expression that can be interpreted in multiple, simultaneous ways. The base can be seen as a sense of vault doors or pages of a book or bridge counter weights or automations. Proportional systems can be devised to interact with the scale of the veins of the marble to create a new and fascinating beauty.

The connecting addition reinterprets the existing building's disposition of elements to reflect its new uses and expression as a modern building while regaining the Federal Reserve's corporate identity. A glass atrium links the two buildings while preserving the bank's original façade.

4   Bridge interior
5   Bridge exterior

5

143

Federal Reserve Bank of Minneapolis Headquarters and Operations Center

Minneapolis, Minnesota, USA

777,000 square feet / 72,185 square meters
Completion: 1995

Architects, planners, and landscape architects worked together to design this headquarters and operations center along the banks of the Mississippi River.

The project reconnected pedestrians to the river and downtown Minneapolis, restored an important public plaza, and highlighted the historical significance of the location, which was the site of Minneapolis's original settlement and first public square.

1

2

1   Beacons at Bridgehead Square

2   Mississippi River overlook

3   Bridgehead Plaza

The headquarters building consists of two structures: a seven-story office tower and a four-story, terraced operations center. The structures are connected by an outdoor courtyard and underground and above-ground passageways.

The landscaped plaza, which is overlooked by the curved glass wall of the main headquarters building, includes a 222-foot clock tower, a City Art Map and a public green space that provides five interpretive displays about the site's history.

3

Florida Aquarium

Tampa, Florida, USA

152,000 square feet / 14,121 square meters

Completion: 1995

Joint venture partners: EHDD (Esherick, Homsey, Dodge & Davis)
and Joseph A. Wetzel Associates, Inc., exhibit designers

1

The Florida Aquarium tells the story of Florida's diverse water habitats—from
stream and swamp to coast and open sea—in an educational and entertaining
way, while inspiring in visitors a sense of stewardship for the aquatic environment.
The scheme provides enclosures for the marine animal and plant exhibits, as well
as for free-flying birds, in a design that reflects the site's maritime surroundings.

A prominent shell-shaped glass dome covers the Florida Wetlands exhibit, ensuring that sufficient daylight is available to sustain native Florida habitats under near-natural conditions. The sail-shaped canopies on the building exterior provide shade while evoking maritime images of the surrounding bay.

Other aquarium spaces are designed to create an architectural flow from the entry, giving visitors a dramatic sense of rising up and winding through the exhibit layers of marine life, plants, and free-flying birds.

The two major habitat stories are organized around a large public lobby. This space serves as a reception and access area for the restaurant and retail shop and orientation space for visitors before and after experiencing the exhibits. The second level of the lobby provides ready access to concessions as well as to outdoor terraces and children's outdoor exhibits.

1   Exterior view

2   Interior of glass dome

3   Detail of glass dome

4   Glass detail

2

3

4

1

Florida International University
Patricia & Philip Frost Art Museum

Miami, Florida, USA

46,000 square feet / 4,275 square meters
Completion: 2008

1   Knife edge at north end of grand galleries

2   Site plan

This museum is the new cultural heart of the campus.
It houses artwork from the university's permanent
collection, hosts temporary exhibitions, and presents
educational programs and symposia. The museum
includes 11,000 square feet (1,015 square meters)
of galleries, a lecture hall, a shop, and a café.

The structure features a soaring three-story glass atrium
entrance and a dramatically suspended staircase leading
to the second- and third-floor exhibition spaces. The
design includes skylights that allow the museum to exhibit
many of the works in natural light. All ultraviolet light is
filtered out, and light levels and colors are carefully
controlled by an array of large "petals" that preferentially
scatter light to the walls.

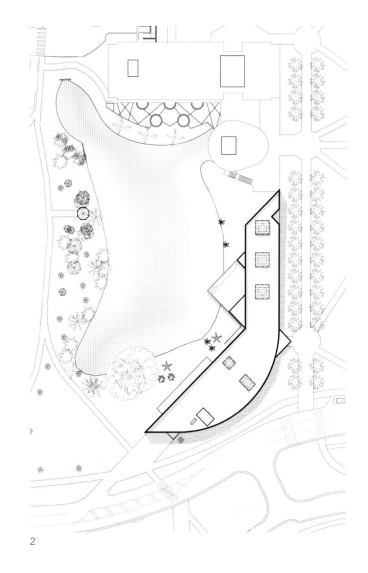

2

3

3   View from west across lake

4   Level 1 floor plan

5   Level 2 floor plan

6   Level 3 floor plan

7   View into UV-filtering skylight
    through array of light-scattering
    optical "petals"

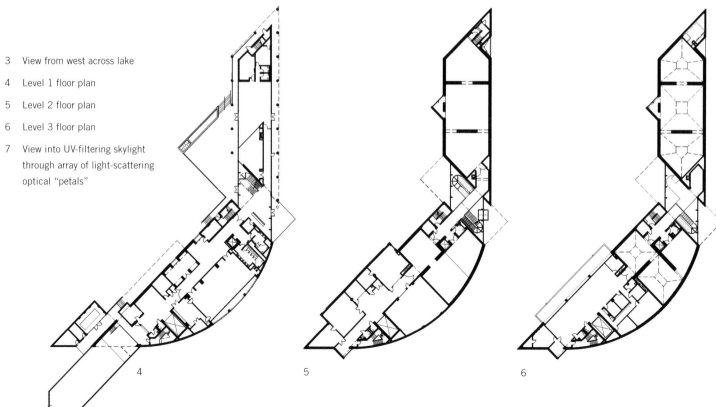

4   5   6

Foreign & Commonwealth Office, Whitehall
London, UK

1 million square feet / 93,000 square meters
Completion: 1997

1   Secretary of State's office

2   Staircase and ceiling detail

1

Retaining the character of the original 1870s Victorian construction while creating one of the UK's most technologically advanced buildings was the challenge for the Foreign & Commonwealth Office refurbishment.

The refurbishment plan recognizes the clear distinction between the Office's political departments, which respond to world events, and its support services, which have predetermined and ongoing technological requirements. The design creates accommodation efficiencies that enable all departments to consolidate operations onto a single site.

2

3   Atrium

4   Façade

4

Working with English Heritage and specialist conservators, significant historical and architectural elements were identified and restored to their original appearance. Discreet use of original materials, colors, and building techniques retains the historic character and harmonizes new and old elements. Spaces of the highest architectural or historical significance, known as the Fine Areas, were fully researched using both existing records and on-site investigative techniques. These areas were restored to their original appearance wherever possible.

A phased program spanning 17 years allowed occupants to remain on site and operations to continue without interruption.

The project was awarded the prestigious Europa Nostra Medal of Honour for the meticulous detailing work.

Forest Park Jewel Box Grounds

St. Louis, Missouri, USA

17 acres / 7 hectares
Completion: 2005

Situated at the high point of a ridge, the art deco Jewel Box building commands a site that includes open woods, lawns, and gardens that fall away in all four directions. Built in 1936, the 50-foot-tall glass and steel conservatory is listed on the National Register of Historic Places; the three formal reflecting pools at its south side are also listed as contributing site structures.

The master plan design reestablishes the site as a park destination. It respects the site's historical significance while creating better site connections and enhanced attractions that increase its use.

Inspiring the new plan are ideas of light, water, plants, and movement embodied in the original conception of the Jewel Box. Lighting animates the building, water features, and site elements at night. Water is a unifying element that moves through the landscape. Plantings define spaces, movement, and views while providing a changing seasonal palette. Gardens east of the building are framed by a tree-lined promenade and great lawn to the south. A linear glass and steel trellis structure on the north side leads to an airy glass and steel pavilion set in the middle of the enlarged lagoon.

2

1   Site plan, landscape gardens, and grounds

2   Pavilion on the lake

40 Grosvenor Place

London, UK

325,000 square feet / 30,195 square meters
Completion: 1999

1   Entrance

2   Forum with clear-span stepped glazing

1

Property owner and developer Grosvenor believes the office of the future must be energy-efficient, socially responsible, and flexible. For this speculative office project in London's Belgravia neighborhood, Grosvenor wanted a modern building that would thrive in the local market while accommodating different users over the next 200–300 years.

The design incorporates an integrated mix of community tenant uses surrounding a large atrium. This landscaped, naturally ventilated atrium contributes light to the building's upper levels while providing access to a restaurant, conference center, health club, convenience retail, and a concierge, and offering separate entrances for up to four tenants. A covered, street-level internal route through the building provides access from Hobart Place to Grosvenor Place.

2

3

3   Atrium from fourth-level walkway

4   Section

5   First floor plan

6   Rear steelwork detail

6

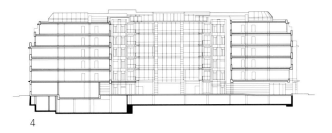
4

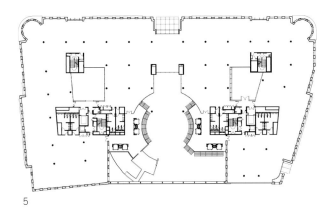
5

The structure of the building is distinctive in its combination of a cast-in-place concrete frame with a precast bearing wall perimeter. The elimination of the structure's perimeter columns gave flexibility to the space planning process and contributed to the building's energy-efficient performance. A typical office floor has no workspace more than 25 feet (7.6 meters) from natural light. The natural light is enhanced by translucent glass mullions that eliminate solar gain while reflecting light deep into the plan.

The exterior features a high-performance façade of natural limestone and glass designed to complement the surrounding historic buildings, which include Buckingham Palace.

The British Council for Offices named 40 Grosvenor Place the "Best Commercial Workplace in Britain" in 2001.

1

Franchise Tax Board Offices

Sacramento, California, USA

1 million square feet / 92,900 square meters
Completion: 2005

1   Central courtyard

2   Perforated sunscreens on west façade

3   Wall section at sunscreens

2

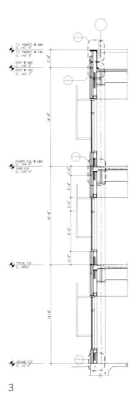

3

This facility improves the comfort and productivity of 7,500 Franchise Tax Board employees. The expansion added two large office buildings, a warehouse and a "town center." Open to the public and focused around a tree-shaded plaza and busy light rail station, the town center provides dining, daycare, training/ meeting rooms, a sundries store, a lecture hall, and other amenities.

The main pedestrian circulation is organized around a garden courtyard that connects all buildings. Cafés, break rooms, stairs, and conference rooms are located along this pedestrian street.

The buildings reflect the State of California's commitment to sustainable building practices and include a variety of sustainable strategies. The buildings perform 20 percent better than required by California Title 24 Energy Standards and have achieved LEED Silver certification.

1

Fukuoka International Airport
International Passenger Terminal
Fukuoka, Japan

710,000 square feet / 66,000 square meters
Completion: 1999
Associate architects: Azusa Sekkei, Mishima Architects, and MHS Planners

1   Departure lobby

2   Departure drop-off

This international passenger terminal in northwestern Japan was designed as a new "gateway to Asia." The terminal integrates lightweight, simple-span structures and north-facing clerestories to provide spectacular views of nearby mountains.

The gently curved roof is divided into five airfoil-like shells that hover above the main departure level. Like wings of an airplane taking off, the leading edges are lifted toward the airside, capturing north light and glimpses of the sky for passengers in the ticketing areas on the departure

2

3

level. The supporting structure is exposed tube steel that together forms lines of floor-to-ceiling composite trusses, running east–west under the clerestories. This design allows for large 33-foot (10-meter) overhangs on the east and west, as well as a column-free spine in the center. The skylight spine features a distinctive, atrium-like midsection where travelers are able to move about freely. Serving as the main circulation hub, the atrium symbolizes the connection between land and sky, linking Fukuoka to other ports in Asia.

3   Concession concourse
4   Airside view

4

Georgia Archives
Morrow, Georgia, USA

172,000 square feet / 15,980 square meters
Completion: 2003

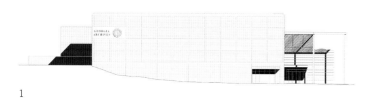

1

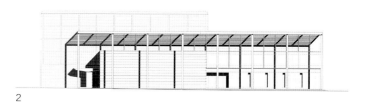

2

This building houses Georgia's historical records and documents dating back to colonial times. Balancing stringent technological and security requirements with a visually striking, comfortable environment, the design creates a light, open building that provides an exceptional setting for information sharing.

The building orientation and geometry were designed to be responsive to solar and site conditions. Wrapping compact stacked vaults with laboratory and office spaces reduces the building envelope, reducing energy use and

1   North elevation

2   West elevation

3   Oculus detail

3

4

5

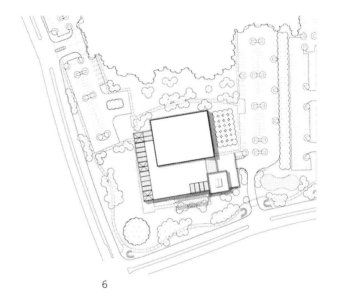

6

creating a more stable environment to protect the important historical collection. The design meets strict security and environmental conditions while inviting the community to explore the treasured records housed within.

Notable features include pervasive natural light tempered with high-performance glass, sunscreens, and porches. Reinterpreting the classic oculi common in traditional Southern civic architecture, the lobby's circular skylights draw in light and provide a glimpse of the portico sunshades above. The focal point is a two-story lobby and public display gallery constructed of reclaimed heart-of-pine.

4 Dusk exterior

5 First-floor walkway

6 Site plan

171

Guy Carpenter Headquarters
New York, New York, USA

125,000 square feet / 11,610 square meters
Completion: 2003

1   Work stations

2   Executive area

2

While its new space needed to be upscale enough to support visits from executive-level clients, Guy Carpenter didn't want the design to portray the image of a traditional insurance company.

The design creates a predominantly open-plan environment for more than 350 Guy Carpenter employees on the fourth floor of the former Met Life building at One Madison Avenue. The building's 125,000-square-foot (11,600-square-meter) floor plate takes up a full city block and is 430 feet (130 meters) long.

The non-linear interior plan makes the vast space more intimate by creating a series of small, connected neighborhoods. A sweeping, curved "main street" with

3

different vistas along the route masks the support columns and guides people through the space. The color palette is neutral, and the design creates a high–low rhythm by varying the heights of workstation panels.

Except for conference rooms and enclosed offices, the space has no ceilings. A suspended canopy of translucent screens imprinted with bare trees brings a feeling of nature into the space. The sail-like panels improve acoustics while serving as an attractive wayfinding element.

The executive and client areas have a more "corporate" feel, with wood accents and larger enclosed offices. The executive space includes a boardroom and customer dining area.

3   Community area

4   Reception area

4

Hampton Roads Convention Center

Hampton, Virginia, USA

344,000 square feet / 31,960 square meters
Completion: 2005

1

2

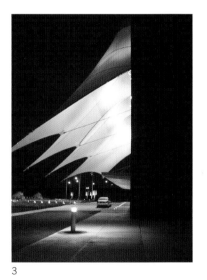

3

The contemporary design of the Hampton Roads Convention Center draws inspiration from the nautical roots of the Hampton community. Topped by a dramatic tensile roof, it features a 108,000-square-foot (10,033-square-meter) exhibit hall, a 28,000-square-foot (2,600-square-meter) ballroom, an intimate conference center, and 35 flexible meeting spaces.

4

1 Plaza light detail

2 Channel glass tower

3 Tensile structure night view

4 Exhibit hall entrances

The prominent white tensile structure, covered with Teflon-coated fiberglass, suggests the form of a sail. Along with three adjacent channel glass towers, it provides an anchor while adding interest to the expanse of the long, horizontal building. The sail-like form also provides a modern interpretation of the historic city of Hampton, which was founded in 1610.

5   Fountain at ballroom drop-off

6   Tensile structure

6

The designers oriented the building and its glazed elevations to the south and made extensive use of shading devices to provide daylighting and views to the interior while minimizing summer solar heat gain. The transition between the indoor and the outdoor environment is modulated by the tensile structure, which covers the drop-off and ballroom terrace and provides partial enclosure for outdoor activities during mild weather. Its translucence allows a softened daylight to enter the building, which is dramatically punctuated by direct sunlight from the four oculi. The transition from the semi-enclosed space of the tensile structure to the full enclosure of the lobby is modulated by skylights and fabric panels on the lobby ceiling.

Though the building is on an urban site, a large lake and the adjacent Hampton Roads Coliseum are important thematic elements. A series of water walls, fountains, jets, and pools link indoor and outdoor spaces, connecting buildings and activities while mediating between the built and natural environment.

5

179

Harlem Hospital Center
Master Plan and Patient Pavilion
New York, New York, USA

150,000 square feet / 13,935 square meters
Completion: 2004

1   Art murals

2   Proposed exterior façade

1

This major modernization at Harlem Hospital Center integrates inpatient, emergency room, and outpatient services in a new Patient Pavilion, to create one unified healthcare complex and a landmark that reflects Harlem's unique cultural heritage.

Included in the modernization plan is the restoration of priceless art murals, which will become the centerpiece of the design and the inspiration for the new face of the hospital. The proposed design for the new pavilion features a lobby gallery, in which the historic murals will be displayed, visible to passersby. The fritted-glass five-story façade will feature imagery replicated from the hospital's WPA-era murals, creating an identity for the hospital and engaging patients and the wider community.

Indianapolis International Airport
Col. H. Weir Cook Terminal
Indianapolis, Indiana, USA

1.2 million square feet / 111,480 square meters
Completion: 2008
Architect of Record: AeroDesign Group

1

1 Terminal at dusk

2 Terminal plan

3 Interior columns

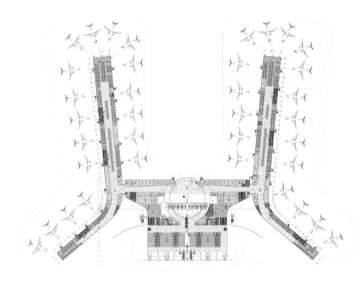

2

This glass-and-steel, dual-level midfield terminal features two concourses, 40 passenger gates, retail space for restaurants and shopping, and state-of-the-art security, passenger conveyance, and baggage handling facilities. The focal point of the terminal is Civic Plaza, a monumental, 200-foot-diameter central hall, serving as a grand arrival and departure space that reflects the art, history, and culture of Indianapolis. It is the country's first sustainable, post-9/11, greenfield air terminal.

The structure is shaped by a response to the natural environment. Visitors can see out the five-story window wall and connect to the landscape. High-performance glass curtain walls enclose the building, with the roof acting as a broad shelter that shades the activities within the terminal while drawing in natural light through semi-opaque skylights. The swooping roofline creates a symbolic gateway to the region.

3

4

James J. Stukel Towers and UIC Forum
University of Illinois
Chicago, Illinois, USA

500,000 square feet / 46,450 square meters
Completion: 2007 (Stukel Housing); 2008 (Forum)

1

2

UIC's new mixed-use development has created a unique identity for the university's South Campus in downtown Chicago. The design embodies the relationship between student life, academic enrichment, and social and convocation requirements in an urban campus setting.

The centerpiece is James Stukel Towers, a residence hall for 740 students that is composed of four towers of different heights. Each two-story community shares a comfortable two-story commons area and each tower has a penthouse lounge/piano room.

3

The project includes a 3,000-seat convocation center ("The Forum"), a 150-seat event center, student study room spaces, computer labs, a full-service dining hall for residents, and retail tenants.

The development encourages students to spend more time on campus while providing social venues that attract people from the wider community. The prominent location provides stunning views to and from the campus.

4

3   Southeast view of Forum entrance

4   South view of Forum pre-function area

5   Ground floor and site plan

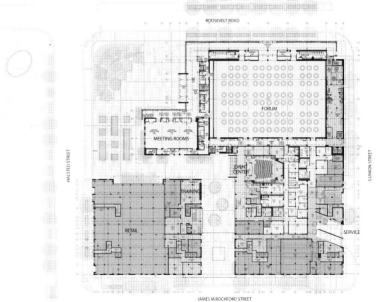
5

JWT Offices

Chicago, Illinois, USA

50,000 square feet / 4,645 square meters
Completion: 2004

1   Seating area

2   Lobby area

Chicago's oldest advertising firm wanted its new offices to reinvigorate its brand and identity. The design incorporates this rebranding and a vibrant color palette while supporting the agency's work processes.

JWT's new identity begins on the first floor, as visitors are guided up a private escalator to reception. Along the way they are exposed to the inner workings of the advertising studio and dynamic flat screens running JWT campaigns. The reception area incorporates waiting space, a café, meeting space, and conference facilities.

1

2

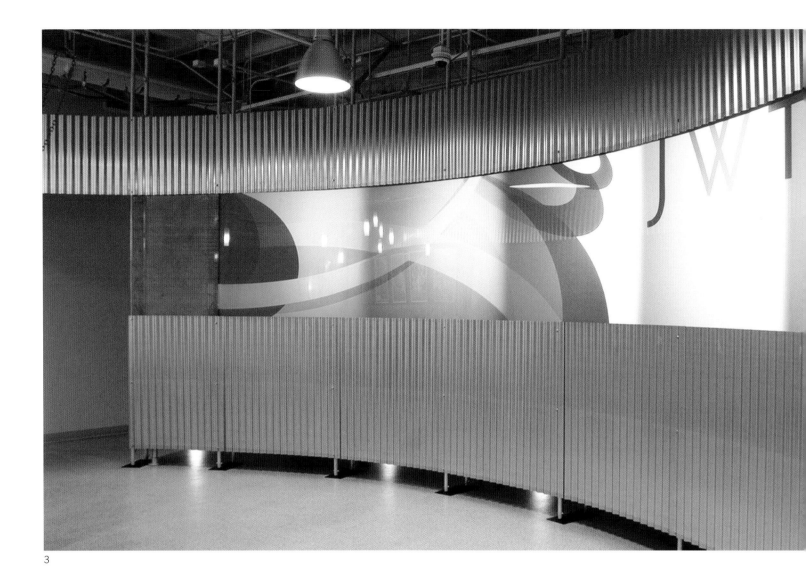

3

3   Graphics at reception

4   Reception

4

Workstations are designed with parts and pieces on casters so that as employees collaborate and create teams, they can easily move their belongings. The space includes a focus group room with a residential feel and a one-way mirror, high-tech production studios, and a creative lounge that is based on an Amsterdam coffee house.

1

Kai Tak Archipelago Master Plan

Hong Kong, China

740 acres / 300 hectares
Completion: 2004

The aim of this master plan for the redevelopment of the vacated Kai Tak airport is to increase community access to Hong Kong's highly desirable waterfront.

The master plan celebrates the site's aviation heritage by converting the runway into an archipelago of spectacular island neighborhoods. At the end of the residential island chain, accessed by ferry, tram, and cycling paths, is a cultural destination that commemorates Kai Tak's aviation history.

A vast waterfront park carries the harborside character of open vistas deep into the surrounding community, enhancing real estate value and creating a catalyst for redeveloping neighboring industrial areas into new commercial centers.

1   Aerial view

2   Illustrative plan

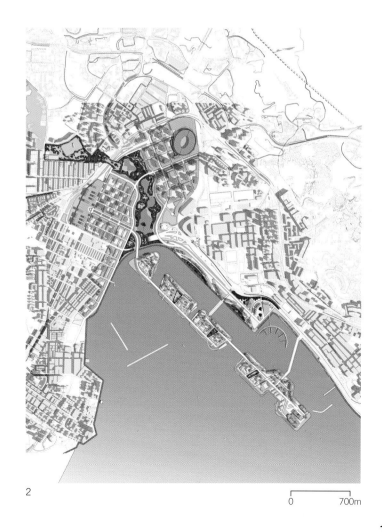

2

0   700m

Kellogg Corporate Headquarters

Battle Creek, Michigan, USA

510,000 square feet / 47,380 square meters
Completion: 1986

1 Site plan

2 Landscaping detail

3 Landscaped entry plaza

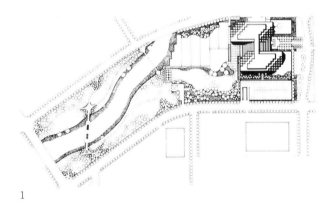

1

A headquarters of warm red brick, creamy limestone, pale-green glass, and teakwood on a 17-acre, carefully landscaped river site befits a company whose very essence is agrarian.

The central skylit atrium with its bridges and escalators, rich woods framing private offices and special facilities, and artwork inspired by agricultural themes create an atmosphere of light and warmth for Kellogg employees.

2

3

Kent County Courthouse
Warwick, Rhode Island, USA

200,000 square feet / 18,600 square meters
Completion: 2006

1   South elevation

2   Glass sail

1

The transparent façade of this new courthouse building expresses the openness and accessibility of the modern judicial process. Distinctly Modernist in design, the courthouse relates to its New England site, and to the maritime history and culture of Rhode Island through the use of reinterpreted traditional red brick and limestone masonry details juxtaposed with large glass wall surfaces. An abstract glass sail houses the main vertical circulation.

The theme of transparency extends to the public waiting area, which features all-glass spaces that offer a glimpse into the public processes taking place inside. The interior emphasizes light and air circulation and features improved accessibility and generous spaces.

2

Kiener Plaza

St. Louis, Missouri, USA

2 acres / 0.8 hectare

Plan completion: 2008

1   Site plan

2   Overall site perspective

Kiener Plaza is in the heart of downtown St. Louis and is an important part of the linear Gateway Mall that reaches from the grounds of the iconic Gateway Arch and runs 10 blocks to the west.

The design incorporates an innovative shade and performance structure, representing a commitment to sustainability. The plaza and solar structure act not only as dynamic forms, but also as an outward sign of the progressive nature of Saarinen's Arch and the city of St. Louis. The structure will serve as the main lighting source for the plaza and as the backdrop to culturally significant presentations and concerts. It has the potential to power light installations in the downtown community.

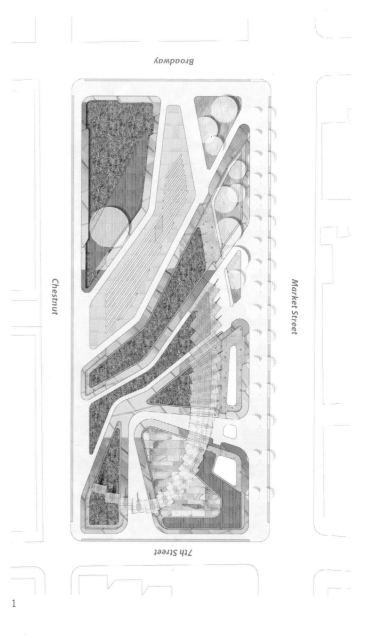

1

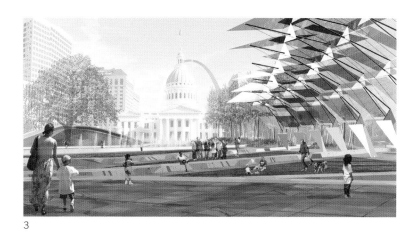

3

4

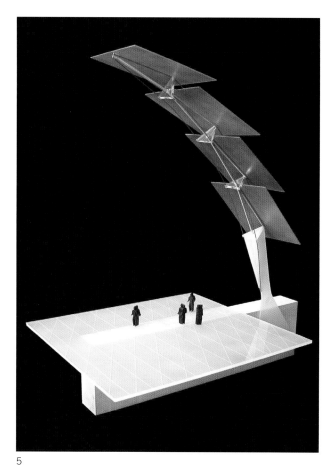

5

3 Courthouse perspective

4 Chestnut Street/Gateway Arch perspective

5 Architecture as sculpture

6 Concert perspective from top of hill pavilion

Three layers of interventions were devised to bring an urban quality to the massing of the parking structures adjacent to the plaza. First, street-level shops and restaurants could be reprogrammed and physically reconfigured to appear as multi-story façades that relate to the civic scale of the space they front. Second, the remaining south-facing façades of the garages are to be

6

covered in a veil formed by a tightly woven stainless-steel mesh with integral LED lights that together act as a large-scale digital display. This surface would interact with the "solar" sculpture to create an engaging and symbolic space. Finally, a thin layer of offices and special rooftop café/bars would activate the roofscape of the garage.

Killbear Provincial Park Visitor Centre

Noble, Ontario, Canada

12,000 square feet / 1,115 square meters
Completion: 2006

1

1   West entrance

2   Main entrance at dusk

With dramatic views of Georgian Bay along the Great Lakes Heritage Coast in northern Ontario, this visitor center fits within the rugged landscape in a way that celebrates and respects the natural environment and its ecosystems.

The design created a facility that is strongly connected to its site in form and organization, enhancing the visitor

3

4

experience through the introduction of natural light and the careful orchestration of views. The building melds with the site by stretching out parallel to a series of rock folds that cascade toward the water's edge, while its volumes twist and overlap like the rocks themselves. The east and west elevations lean away from the water's edge like an eastern white pine gnarled by the wind. The building shifts, cants, twists, and slopes like the surrounding rocky terrain, connecting visitors with the landscape as they journey through the exhibits.

3   Viewing deck
4   Mezzanine west ramp

5

Sustainable design strategies include using the nearby Georgian Bay waters as a heating and cooling source, using stormwater runoff to maintain wetlands of indigenous plant species, and using recycled and recyclable building materials.

5   Front entry detail

6   Front entry

6

King Abdullah University of Science and Technology

Rabigh, Saudi Arabia

6.5 million square feet / 603,870 square meters
Completion (university): 2009

2

1   Master plan of KAUST campus

2   Solar tower

The new King Abdullah University of Science and Technology (KAUST) is a world-class graduate research university and town center built on the western coast of Saudi Arabia, approximately 50 miles north of Jeddah on the Red Sea.

The campus proper is located at the center of the surrounding development. Its gateway is the administration building, which establishes a primary east–west axis that terminates at the harbor. The academic and research institutes are organized along three secondary north–south axes that form the primary circulation network. These axes connect the campus to the commercial center, providing direct access into the heart of the campus.

3

Two of the three axes, or spines, are covered pedestrian streets that lead to different research institutions. These areas include a public zone with conference and exhibition facilities and an auditorium, as well as a private zone for future research incubator buildings. The third spine provides vehicular access to underground parking and building services, as well as an at-grade connection between the commercial center, mosque, and campus quadrangle.

The design combines centuries-old practices for sustainability and comfort with the latest energy-saving and energy-producing technologies. Two dozen individual buildings are clustered under a single roof covered by energy-generating photovoltaics.

3   Campus entry
4   Laboratory entry court

4

5

6

Shaded walkways and gathering places promote collegial idea-sharing. Additional sustainable technologies used include solar chimneys, heat recovery wheels, innovative façades and shading techniques, and high-efficiency glazing. Twin towers powered by solar cells transform water from the Red Sea into a fine mist that cools the campus. The design recycles condensate, gray water, black water, and stormwater for all on-site irrigation needs.

The plan protects the Red Sea and its fragile mangrove lagoons. A spectacular coral-reef ecosystem is being preserved for use as a marine sanctuary and research area.

5   Central quadrangle and library

6   Library, laboratories, and seacourt at dusk

7   Laboratories

7

King's Library at the British Museum

London, UK

21,500 square feet / 2,000 square meters
Completion: 2003

1   View from north door

2   Restored book presses

Originally completed in 1827, the King's Library presented an enormous challenge when its collection of books moved to the British Library and left the room without a function. To make the space itself the primary attraction, the project created a discrete exhibition area with few interventions to the historic fabric.

Working from historical records and drawings, the designers revitalized the magnificent room. Conservation of the ceilings, book presses, floors, and wall surfaces has restored the splendor of the original decorative scheme. The revival of an old style of exhibition for the museum—the Cabinet of Curiosities—further enhances the architecture.

1

Kingwood College Health & Science Building

Kingwood, Texas, USA

77,000 square feet / 7,155 square meters
Completion: 2004

1

1 Main entrance

2 View from main entrance
   looking east to campus

This building acts as a bridge between the original campus
quadrangle and the recently completed Student Services
Building. Its scale and materials palette acknowledge
the competing styles while establishing a new campus
aesthetic for future development. The exterior façade
is predominantly banded brick with recessed windows.

2

3

4

3   Lobby

4   Entrance from southeast at dusk

The main lobby is a two-and-a-half story atrium covered with a large overhanging canopy roof that creates a shaded porch for students. This atrium space extends visually to the commons area through a clear glass curtainwall.

The facility houses the chemistry, geology, biology, and physics/astronomy departments within the Natural Sciences Program, and the nursing, respiratory, occupational therapy, and dental hygiene departments within the Health Program. It contains classrooms, science and computer labs, lecture halls, offices, and a central storage area.

London Marriott West India Quay Tower

London, UK

1 million square feet / 93,000 square meters
Completion: 2004

1   Level 32 floor plan

2   View across dock

3   Finish detail

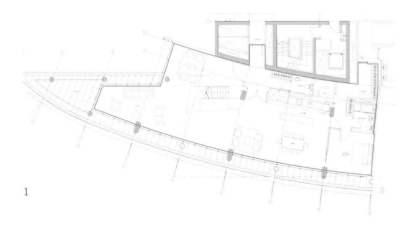

1

2

This hotel and apartment tower is at West India Quay, adjacent to the Canary Wharf Estate in London's Docklands. It includes 158 luxury apartments, 47 serviced apartments, and 12 stories of hotel rooms and suites.

The tight urban site, dual-use cores, complex ground conditions, and challenging occupancy requirements presented many design opportunities.

3

Rising above the vibrant Canary Wharf district, this 32-story glass and aluminum-clad high-rise reflects the neighboring towers. Its sweeping curve echoes the water's edge.

The terracotta podium, which relates to the nearby Victorian warehouse residential conversions, contains restaurants, bars, banquet halls, and other public areas.

4

5

6

4　Podium and finish detail

5　Glass wall

6　Interior view from penthouse

Maricopa County Fourth Avenue Jail

Phoenix, Arizona, USA

541,000 square feet / 50,260 square meters
Completion: 2004
Associate architect: Durrant Architects

1   Elevation detail

2   South elevation

3   Site plan

2

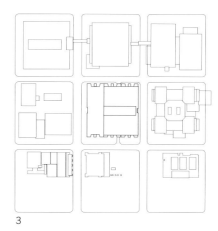

3

This four-story maximum-security jail is the central booking jail for Maricopa County and accommodates more than 2,000 inmates. The building is compressed into one city block in downtown Phoenix, and adheres to a strict height limitation.

In response to its context—Phoenix's historic railroad warehouse district—the building is clad in materials including brick, glass block, stainless-steel panels, and pre-cast concrete lintels. Keeping the mass low and horizontal further emphasizes the "warehouse" concept. Simple and effective brick detailing and coursing humanizes the scale by creating shadow lines on the façade.

MasterCard Global Technology and Operations Headquarters

O'Fallon, Missouri, USA

550,000 square feet / 52,000 square meters
Completion: 2001

1   Reception area

2   Double-height promenade

MasterCard's Global Technology and Operations Headquarters houses all the company's local employees under one roof. The facility features office space, a call center, secure data center, and cafeteria.

The three four-story office buildings have open 35,000-square-foot (3,250-square-meter) floor plates. This universal space gives MasterCard flexibility to easily reconfigure its work environments to accommodate technology and business changes.

An internal "main street" runs along an 8-acre (3-hectare) lake; offices are located to provide maximum access to lake views.

2

McGuire Woods LLP Law Offices

Century City, California, USA

50,000 square feet / 4,645 square meters
Completion: 2006

1   View of reception desk

2   View of reception area with interconnecting stair

3   Detail of reception area with Markus Linnenbrink painting

1

2

The law offices of McGuire Woods, in three stories of a Century City high-rise, have a modern yet classic feeling. Judicious use of rich finishes such as stone, glass, and wood in the primarily painted gypsum-board environment complements the firm's image.

A dramatic, custom-designed stone, wood, and glass staircase combines with a tiered ceiling to help compensate for the lack of exterior views. The library is at one corner of the building. The stacks recede dramatically as they move toward the reading lounge at the point. Glass-walled conference rooms are positioned on corners adjacent to the reception area.

3

1

MedImmune Research and Office Campus

Gaithersburg, Maryland, USA

210,000 square feet / 19,510 square meters
Completion: 2001

1 Open stair in atrium

2 First floor plan

3 Entry canopy

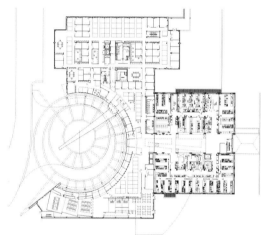

2

3

MedImmune's headquarters provides office, research space, and amenities for almost 600 employees in a campus-style facility. The interior environment reflects progressive thinking and the company's tradition by blending classic quality and modern technology.

The design intent was to create a single building that improves communication between the research group and the rest of the organization. The atrium spaces, communal areas, and open staircases promote collaboration. Locating the atrium, café, library, conference rooms, and break-out

4

spaces along the intersections between the laboratory and administrative areas increases opportunities for interaction.

The flexible building configuration enables MedImmune to add modules of office or laboratory space as the company grows.

5

Missouri Historical Society Expansion and Renovation

St. Louis, Missouri, USA

129,000 square feet / 11,984 square meters
Completion: 1999

1   Lobby joining expansion with existing museum

2   Detail

The primary design considerations for this museum addition were to connect the natural setting of St. Louis's Forest Park with the urban edge along the city street, and to enable the Missouri Historical Society to expand its services and deepen its relationship with the community. The building sits on a traffic circle that acts as a major entry to Forest Park. Its classic columns and limestone face create a monumental gateway.

The renovation and expansion triples the size of the existing Jefferson Memorial Building while maintaining the museum's original north–south axis and breaking the

2

3

building down into discrete zones projecting south into the park. The expanded facility houses local and regional history exhibitions, expanded collaboration activities, discussion spaces for community-based programming, a 350-seat auditorium, a restaurant, and a museum shop.

The addition used technology to accomplish the Society's goals for an environmentally friendly design that conserves resources for the future. Building systems were designed to maximize natural light, ventilation, and energy efficiency. The exterior cladding is a regionally manufactured, pre-cast concrete panel that is a durable, low-cost, and low-maintenance material.

4

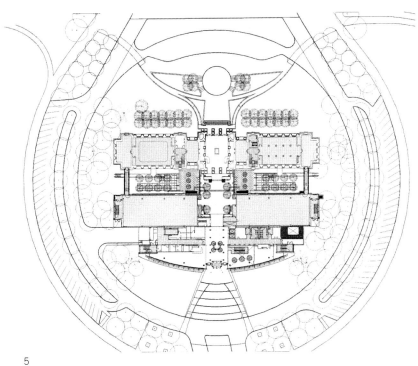

5

3   East façade

4   South entrance

5   Site plan

Motorola Executive Offices Renovation

Schaumburg, Illinois, USA

18,000 square feet / 1,670 square meters
Completion: 2005

2

1   Waiting area

2   Reception area

Motorola's renovated executive floor offices are on the 12th floor of a 1970s office building in suburban Chicago. The design reflects the image of an energetic, high-technology company that is moving "fast forward."

To help drive Motorola's culture from hierarchical to more egalitarian, a new company-wide 15- by 15-foot interior office standard was applied to all the executive areas, including the CEO's office.

The renovated space includes a state-of-the-art conference center open to all employees.

National Air and Space Museum

Washington, DC, USA

630,000 square / 58,530 square meters
Completion: 1976

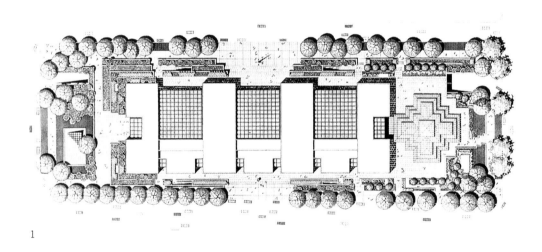

1

Creating a suitable complement to its neighbors, which include the United States Capitol and the National Gallery of Art, was the main design consideration for the National Air and Space Museum (NASM). Celebrating the United States' remarkable achievements in flight, the NASM houses the largest collection of aircraft and spacecraft in the world and ranks among the most-visited museums in the world.

2

3

1 Site plan

2 Night view of main entry

3 Gallery view

4

5

The museum is formed from simple design elements: four
geometric blocks clad in marble matching the exterior of
the National Gallery alternate with three glass-enclosed
exhibit bays. These steel-and-glass bays house the larger
exhibits such as missiles, aircraft, and spacecraft. The
west glass wall of the museum functions as a giant gate,
to allow the installation of airplanes.

4   "Milestones of Flight" gallery

5   Alejandro Otero sculpture

National Air and Space Museum
Steven F. Udvar-Hazy Center

Chantilly, Virginia, USA

708,000 square feet / 65,775 square meters
Completion: 2003

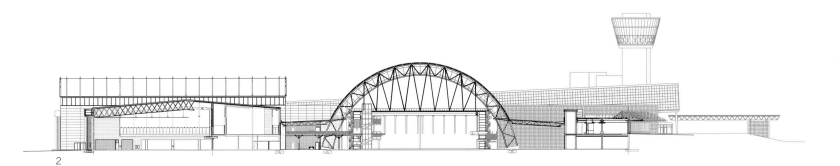

2

1   Night view of main entrance

2   Building section

Following pages:
    Aviation hangar

The design of this museum, located near Dulles Airport, focuses on showcasing its artifacts. The Center is an extension of the original National Air and Space Museum, also designed by HOK.

The aeronautical hangar, 31 meters high and 300 meters long, allows visitors to view aircraft from all perspectives. Visitors can walk among aircraft and small artifacts in display cases located on the floor, and view aircraft hanging from the arched ceiling on elevated skywalks.

The space hangar, on the other hand, is a dark room with direct lighting—much like the high contrast found in outer space—and displays hundreds of famous spacecraft, rockets, satellites and small space-related artifacts.

4

4   Control tower and IMAX theater

5–8   Detail views of façade

The museum's landside contains classrooms, meeting rooms, food courts, gift shops, and an IMAX theater. The airside features a haul road used to access all the hangars. Included is a restoration hangar and craft shops where world-class restoration techniques fulfill the museum's mission of preserving our air and space heritage.

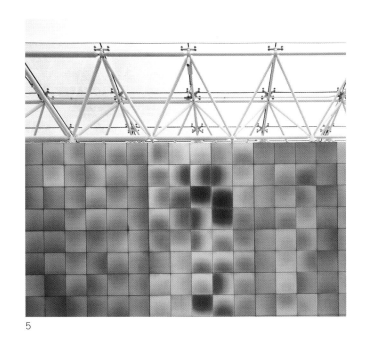

5

6

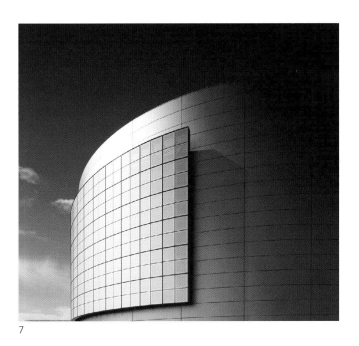

7

8

251

National Wildlife Federation Headquarters

Reston, Virginia, USA

95,000 square feet / 8,825 square meters
Completion: 2000
Project consultant: William McDonough + Partners

1

1   Waterfall at entry

2   View of entry at bridge

The National Wildlife Federation (NWF) headquarters building is adjacent to Lake Fairfax Park in Reston, Virginia. The NWF wanted its new headquarters to reflect its mission by demonstrating sensible stewardship of environmental and financial resources. The design team used a rigorous payback analysis to select "state-of-the-shelf" sustainable technologies and materials.

Native plantings support local wildlife and reduce the need for irrigation and frequent mowing. The building's orientation capitalizes on solar energy sources to reduce energy expenditure and increase natural light. The building's north side, which overlooks the park, is a curtainwall of glass that offers beautiful vistas and floods the spacious interior with welcoming light.

2

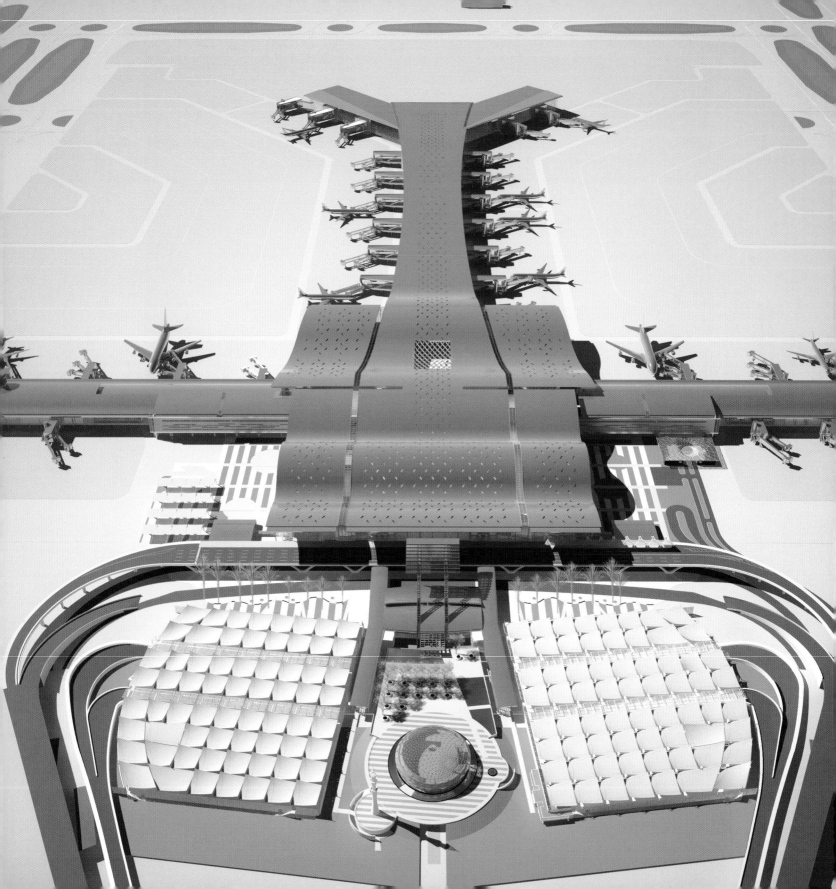

New Doha International Airport

Doha, Qatar

6.3 million square feet / 588,000 square meters
Completion: 2011

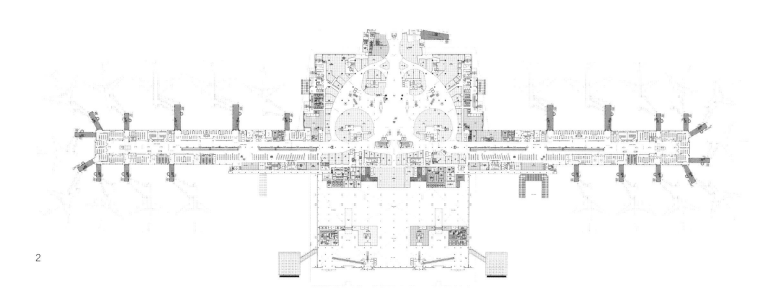

2

1 Bird's-eye view

2 Plan

This passenger terminal complex is rising on reclaimed land adjacent to the Arabian Gulf. Phases 1 and 2 concourses include 40 contact gates plus an additional 10 remote-stand gates.

The project includes a public mosque, a 3,100-car parking garage with an adjacent ground transportation building, two central utility plants, and a flight catering facility. This new airport will be among the first in the world specifically designed to accommodate the new A380-800 Airbus double-decker "super jumbo"—the largest passenger aircraft ever built.

3

NOAA Center for Weather and Climate Prediction

Riverdale Park, Maryland, USA

270,000 square feet / 25,085 square meters
Completion: 2009

1

SOUTH ELEVATION

2

This new office and research complex is the centerpiece of the M-Square Research and Technology Park, adjacent to the University of Maryland in the National Capital Region. Nearly all the meteorological data collected globally will arrive here for analysis by the NOAA's environmental scientists.

The building will house about 750 employees and will be home to NOAA's National Centers for Environmental Prediction, Satellite and Information Service, and Air Resources Laboratory. Locating the facility adjacent to the University of Maryland fosters synergy between NOAA scientists and forecasters and the university's faculty and staff. The environmentally sensitive design, expected to achieve LEED certification, reflects NOAA's mission.

3

1   Model

2   South elevation

3   South façade sunshades

Nortel Brampton Centre

Brampton, Ontario, Canada

1.2 million square feet / 111,483 square meters
Completion: 1996

1   Circulation space

2   Typical "city" street

1

The conversion of a 1963 factory into a high-tech global headquarters provided a framework for communicating Nortel's core values. Recycling the building conserved land, energy, and natural resources and created the opportunity for the company to demonstrate not only its state-of-the-art technology, but also its state-of-the-art ways of working.

A city planning approach breaks down the scale of the high-bay manufacturing space. Boulevards, loops, side streets, alleyways, and shortcuts are marked by color-coded street signs and banners connecting the city's population. Different-sized neighborhoods comprising functional work groups are identified by strong visual elements such as color-coded banners and street signs. A series of piazzas and shops lining the main street help employees integrate work with their daily needs.

2

1

Ogilvy & Mather Offices

Chicago, Illinois, USA

50,000 square feet / 4,645 square meters
Completion: 2005

1 Reception area

2 Floor plan

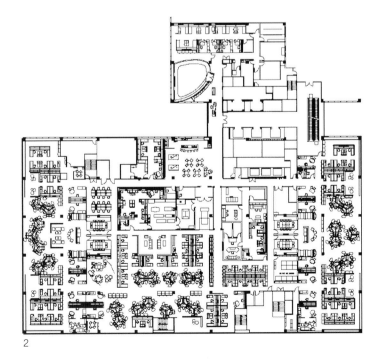

2

Ogilvy & Mather was seeking a dynamic new environment as part of a cultural transformation and consolidation. The firm was operating with a series of private offices split between two floors, an arrangement that hindered collaboration. It wanted space that its people could use as a tool to improve their business.

3

This new office—a renovated apparel center showroom in a redeveloped, 80-year-old high-rise—is bright, light, and egalitarian. The loft-like environment places all employees in open environments, mixing individual workstations with casual settings for impromptu meetings. Sitting together on one floor, creative professionals and account managers can break out of their silos and work as true teams.

3 Open meeting area

4 Circulation

4

The new environment is flexible. Glass-walled conference rooms have aluminum "garage doors" that open to office space and other meeting rooms.

State-of-the-art print and broadcast production studios, which include recording studios and editing stations, are a focal point at the center of the space.

The Ohio State University Medical Center

Columbus, Ohio, USA

3 million square feet / 279,000 square meters
Completion: 2011

1   Building exterior

The new south campus master plan at the University Medical Center includes redevelopment of the James Cancer Hospital and design of a growth strategy for six signature programs: cancer, critical care, heart, neuroscience, imaging, and transplant services.

The design creates a bed tower, new operating and procedural rooms, and radiation therapy, imaging, and outpatient clinic/infusion areas. The project also features parking garages, outdoor green space quadrangles, and new research and education spaces.

1

One McKinley Place

Makati, Philippines

44 stories
Completion: 2001

2

This prestigious residential tower is in the upscale Fort Bonifacio Global City district near Makati City in Manila.

The stylish building comprises two separate towers, joined by a wraparound glass curtain wall and a single two-level podium. The podium contains a restaurant, a business center, swimming pools, amenities, and retail shops. The building responds architecturally to both the site and the geometry of the adjacent fully landscaped gardens and McKinley Park. Two hundred three-bedroom units offer dramatic views of the Fort Bonifacio Global City area and the Manila Golf Course.

1   Building exterior

2   Façade detail

Orange County Groundwater Replenishment System

Orange County, California, USA

Completion: 2008

1   Microfiltration building

Orange County has responded to Southern California's escalating water crisis by building a sophisticated $480-million microfiltration system that transforms wastewater into drinking water. As the world's largest system of its kind, the Groundwater Replenishment System (GRS) supplies purified, high-quality water to half a million Orange County families.

The architectural challenge was to create a character for the campus that would unify the diverse industrial and administrative functions of the GRS while conveying the state-of-the-art functions taking place within.

1

2

2 Transfer pump station

3 Reverse osmosis building

Instead of hiding or "dressing up" the utilitarian industrial systems, the architecture helps tell the story of the entire water purification process to the local community and visitors. The design concept organizes the architectural elements around an indoor–outdoor exhibit path. This linear spine follows the treatment process from effluent to purified water and injection back into the aquifer.

The spine gives the campus an organizational clarity and character that is directly related to the story being told while unifying the various building types. It also gives the facility opportunities to promote recycling, conservation, and other sustainability issues.

This linear concept is an efficient, cost-effective solution that allows the campus to be easily expanded over multiple future phases.

3

Pole Project
Moscow, Russia

12.9 million square feet / 1.2 million square meters
Plan completion: 2008

1 Aerial perspective

This mixed-use development introduces an innovative urban landscape structure that accommodates a diverse population of residents and weaves active retail, commercial, and civic elements into a dynamic whole. The plan integrates a dense urban form with nearby ecosystems.

The development includes 1 million square meters of residential space, 100,000 square meters of commercial space, and 100,000 square meters of public space.

The design uses a block-grid system with four distinct neighborhood blocks that frame the site with a traditional urban structure. The blocks are made up of low- and mid-rise density neighborhoods that incorporate a variety of scales, from large infrastructure elements to intimate pedestrian gardens. The typical six- to eight-story-tall buildings offer standard middle class four-room residences and luxury penthouse apartments. The buildings, framed with windows on all sides, fill the neighborhood blocks by defining the edges of the streets and work together to produce an inviting pedestrian streetscape. Community sky gardens and greenhouses

1

3

2 Northwest neighborhood perspective

3 Hills retail plaza perspective

are incorporated into buildings to access light and nature, repeating the pattern of the unique relationship between the urban composition and natural environment. At the edge of each neighborhood community are live/work spaces that serve as residential units with mezzanines for potential conversion to office or retail space as the district develops. The smaller neighborhoods offer street-front retail and businesses that will include a post office, pharmacy, grocery stores, salon, coffee shops, local police offices, and work spaces.

The site includes 67 hectares of undeveloped land located just outside of the third ring road of Russia's capital. The location, at the edge of the city's metropolitan reach, provides immediate highway access to Moscow's vehicular network. It was historically used for agricultural production and is surrounded by three villages of farmhouses that act as weekend retreats. The site connects to an existing natural forest preserve and a recreational river defines the outer edge of the area, just a short walk to the west side of the development.

4

5

6

4   Park towers perspective

5   Southwest neighborhood perspective

6   Northeast neighborhood perspective

The Priory Chapel

St. Louis, Missouri, USA

25,500 square feet / 2,370 square meters
Completion: 1962

1   Main floor plan

2   Detail

3   Exterior view

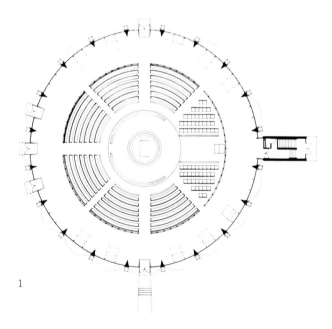

1

Although their tradition was largely rooted in Gothic architecture, the Benedictines of St. Louis wanted to bring a fresh approach to their new home. The Priory Chapel was to be "living" architecture, reflecting the methods, style, and materials of the time.

2

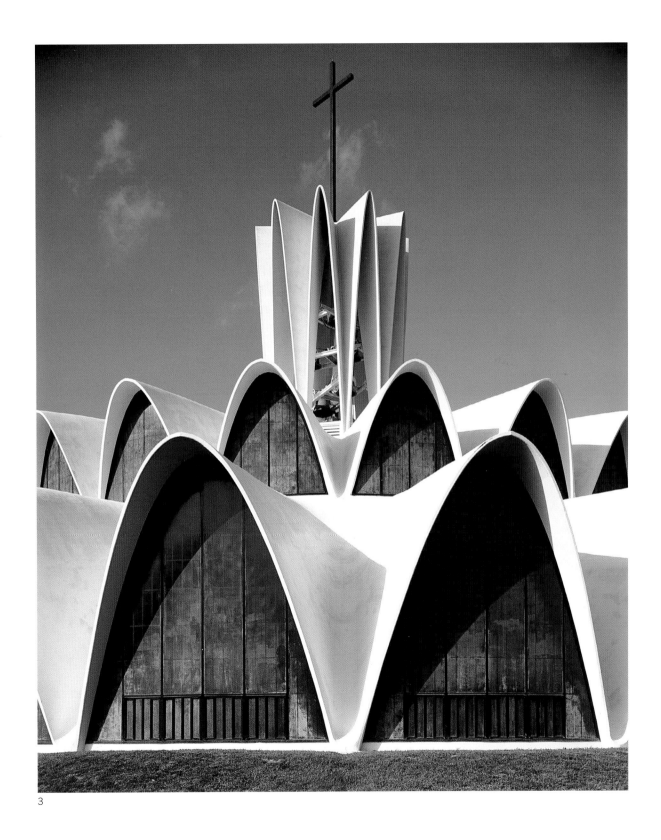

3

4

4 Sanctuary

5 View of illuminated ceiling

6 Interior view of parabolic arch

5

The chapel was designed to accommodate more than 600 people and to create a strong sense of participation among the congregation. Rows of pews encircle the central high altar to draw the entire congregation closer to the officiating priest.

The external shapes consist of three ascending concentric rings of parabolic arches. The first layer of arches, approximately 22 feet high, houses 20 small monastic chapels. An intermediate layer brings light into the nave of the church, and a bell tower with a lantern above the central altar crowns the chapel.

The arches enfold parabolic windows constructed from a double layer of fiberglass, smoke-gray on the exterior and white on the interior. Though they appear black from the outside, the windows admit a soft white glow into the church during the day.

6

Reforma 27 Tower

Mexico City, Mexico

479,000 square feet / 44,500 square meters
Design completion: 2006

1   Amenities aerial front view

2   Reforma Avenue pedestrian view

The reduced front of the building is located in the most important avenue in Mexico City—Paseo de la Reforma—between the "X" and "Y" avenues. This location reduces the impact of the building on pedestrians and of the residents of the building to the busy avenue. The high cost to develop the site dictated a high intensity in the floor use; the resulting design is the architectonic and urban response to these circumstances.

The design places the importance of Paseo de la Reforma to Mexico City in terms of its huge dimensions, urban design, historic symbolism, economic relevance, and extended use for cultural sites and events.

The design locates the building as a participant in the complex configuration of activities that converge on Paseo de la Reforma. At the pedestrian scale, the interior of the building becomes an extension of the street. The front tower features a large opening and sky pool that permits the back tower to have visual contact with the urban environment of Paseo de la Reforma.

2

St. Barnabas Church

Dulwich, UK

10,000 square feet / 929 square meters
Completion: 1995

Following the loss of their 100-year-old Victorian church to a devastating fire, the parish's wish was to create a clear landmark and a welcoming, functional, and adaptable symbol of Christian witness in the community. Parish leaders developed a program for the new church combining expressive aspirational and technical requirements.

The building ultimately constructed is significantly different from early designs, with one exception: the glass spire. The spire's transparent nature reinforces the ancient use of light as a symbol of divine presence, a theme developed throughout the church interior.

The roof's main structure draws in light from above through paired beams, admitting a soft and diffuse light that contrasts with the direct light from windows to the east and west. Eight massive brick piers enclose the space, recalling the old church building while symbolizing the new church and its people—rising up from the earth to light.

1   Sanctuary and choir detail

2   Narthex frames view of the glass spire

2

St. George Intermodal and Cultural Center

Staten Island, New York, USA

209,000 square feet / 19,415 square meters
Completion: 2004

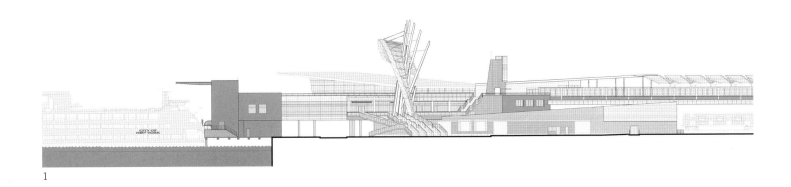

1

The new St. George Intermodal Terminal has transformed the ferry experience for riders and created a state-of-the-art gateway to Staten Island and its waterfront. The architecture integrates sculpture, art, light, and materiality with the building program. The design introduces transparency throughout the building and connectivity back to the water by replacing the former brick walls with new glass curtain walls and increasing ceiling heights by up to 12 feet. The 40-foot-high glass wall alongside the river offers spectacular views of New York Harbor and creates an open and airy environment for waiting passengers.

1   West elevation
2   Water esplanade

2

3   Aerial view

4   Public art "gateway" element

A soaring 350-foot arch supported by 10 cantilevered
columns faces Staten Island and crowns the building.
Inspired by the surrounding bridges, the arched canopy
is lit at night and acts as a powerful beacon for Staten
Island. Sustainable strategies include an 18,000-square-
foot "living roof," rainwater collection, and recycled
building materials.

3

4

St. Louis County Memorial Plaza

Clayton, Missouri, USA

14,000 square feet / 1,300 square meters
Completion: 2000

1

1   Ceremonial processional walk to south

2   Ceremonial processional walk to north

The master plan for the St. Louis County Government campus in Clayton included design of the Police and Firefighter Memorial Plaza and monuments in a new public park dedicated to heroes fallen in the line of duty.

2

3

3   Memorial statuary

4   Grand lawn steps

5   Plinth planters/seating

4

5

In addition to developing an appropriate setting for the urban memorial plaza, the design brought a significant amount of green space into the financial and commercial heart of the city. The project provides a safe, aesthetically pleasing street-level park with fountains, a grass amphitheater, benches, and trees.

Circulation axes between buildings are subtly blended with the procession ways toward the memorial's various elements, forcing awareness and providing a graphic context for the park's use. The central ring reaches "out of bounds" into the city sidewalk, pulling in pedestrians to an unavoidable space. This same ring encloses a raised meadow that is large enough to find a point of isolation at the center, a place for Clayton's residents, employees, and visitors to retreat from the pace of the city.

St. Louis Mississippi Riverfront Master Plan

St. Louis, Missouri, USA

1.5 miles / 2.4 kilometers

Completion: 2006

Joint venture partner: Balmori Associates, New York

1   Site plan

2   View from Eads Bridge

3   Section through riverfront

Located between the river and the grounds of the Gateway Arch and the Jefferson National Expansion Memorial, the project area extends 1.5 miles (2.4 kilometers) along the riverfront. The plan attempts to re-focus the city on the Mississippi River and to complement Eero Saarinen's landmark Arch and Dan Kiley's accompanying monumental landscape.

The riverfront is an integral part of The River Ring, the Great Rivers Greenway District's overall vision for a regional system of interconnected greenways, parks, and trails. As the center of the region, the St. Louis Riverfront will become the hub of the emerging greenway concept.

1

2

3

Preliminary concepts for the Riverfront Plan highlight the city's heritage and its greatest natural resource by reconnecting people with the river.

The plan, which provides a dynamic way of using water and surrounding people with the Mississippi River, includes building a series of islands connected by floating walkways in the river in front of the Arch.

Master plan in association with Balmori Associates in New York

Salvador Dali Museum

St. Petersburg, Florida, USA

75,000 square feet / 6,968 square meters
Completion: 2011

1   View from Bayside Park toward east façade
2   Study of Enigma Hall and spiral stair (rusted steel version)

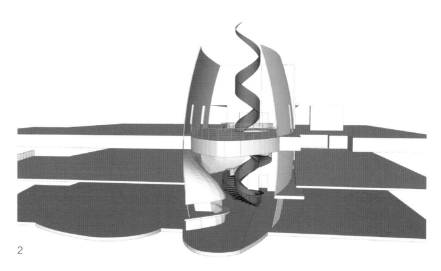

2

The design of this building is symbolic of Surrealism, particularly of Dali's work, and serves as an iconic signal of the importance of the collection within. Visitors will know to expect the extraordinary.

An undulating "enigma" triangulated glass structure forms an organic contrast to the Euclidian mass of the concrete building and shelters the cast-in-place helical staircase connecting the entry hall to the galleries. While the museum design is a secure treasure box that shelters the collection from hurricanes, the design deftly opens up the box to welcome and intrigue visitors.

3

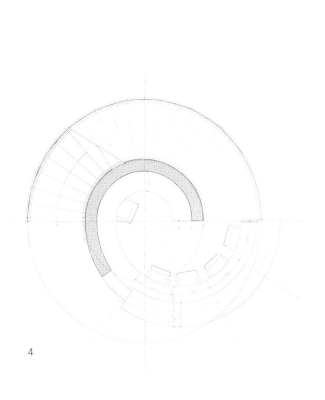

4

5

3   Study of spiral stair (concrete version)

4   Plan view of spiral stair at level 1

5   Level 3 view in Enigma Hall, looking east
     toward balcony overlooking Tampa Bay

The museum has three floors fronting a beautiful waterfront site. It
includes a library, a theater, classroom space, and a community room.

1

Sam M. Gibbons U.S. Courthouse

Tampa, Florida, USA

438,000 square feet / 40,700 square meters
Completion: 1998

1   View up from lobby

2   West façade

Providing an efficient layout and an environmentally sensitive building while complementing an adjacent courthouse were the primary goals directing the design of this new U.S. courthouse. The formal, carefully proportioned design reflects the functions of the spaces inside. Set back from Florida Avenue, the new courthouse creates a pedestrian plaza that mirrors that of the existing courthouse.

The building contains 17 courtrooms, judges' suites, and clerk operation areas. The upper floors house two courts on each floor, as well as judges' chambers. The special proceedings courtroom is on the top floor. The lower six floors provide office and support space.

Natural lighting, passive solar control, environmentally sensitive building materials, and high-efficiency MEP systems are all integral to the energy-conserving design. Building materials were carefully selected to be non-toxic and renewable, and have low embodied energy.

2

1

Samsung Research and Development Campus

Suwon, South Korea

Samsung R3
1.6 million square feet /
148,640 square meters
Completion: 2001

Samsung R4
2.3 million square feet /
213,676 square meters
Completion: 2005

Samsung R5
640,000 square feet / 59,331 square meters
(mid-rise); 670,000 square feet /
62,339 square meters (high-rise)
Completion: 2010 (estimated)

2

The design for each phase of this research and development
campus has been based on Samsung's goals for security,
image, organization, efficiency, flexibility, convenience,
and communication.

1   Bridge to R3
2   Executive floor

3

3   R3 drop-off and main entry

4   R3 south view

Phase 1, the R3 building, has 27 floors with three levels of underground parking and two ground levels due to the slope of the site. In the below-grade portion of the building is a four-level podium that houses public interaction areas, services, employee amenities, and special lab functions that require ground-level access and large floor plates. On top of the podium is a 23-story tower designed with a flexible floor plate to house a variety of combinations of offices and labs. The tower's top levels feature an executive restaurant, boardrooms, and employee amenity facilities.

Phase 2, the R4 building, is a 40-story building that has one semi-below-grade level with a sunken courtyard and four below-grade levels for parking. A six-level podium houses special labs, a multipurpose auditorium, special function spaces, and employee welfare and support functions. Above the podium is a 32-story office tower. Glass curtain walls provide controlled natural light to selected areas of the six-level podium, while modular metal panels clad other parts of the tower. A special labs wing features a sloping glass façade that softens the podium building mass and enhances sunlight penetration.

4

5

Phase 3, the R5 building, gives Samsung flexibility to accommodate future changes. Two alternative schemes, a mid-rise and a high-rise, have been designed to complement buildings R3 and R4 and to advance Samsung's goal of creating a workplace that fosters innovation, creativity, and collaboration.

5   R3 lobby

6   R4 north entry view

6

1

San Bernardino Natural Sciences Annex
California State University

San Bernardino, California, USA

37,500 square feet / 3,485 square meters
Completion: 2005

1 Corner detail

2 Solar screen detail

2

In this science building annex are four clearly different functional spaces: high-tech laboratories and classrooms, a lecture hall, faculty offices, and a museum that features teaching-oriented displays such as fossils, minerals, and collections of animal and plant specimens. Each space is designed to be identified as a self-contained unit, fitting together as a collage of forms and spaces.

The larger-scaled faculty and administration building is an autonomous part of the project, serving as a link to the existing building. Easily distinguishable windows on the laboratory block were designed to symbolize mathematical patterns inspired by the periodic table of elements, and the faculty offices facing north have unobstructed views of the San Bernardino Mountains. This part of the campus helps promote a community connection through a series of public museums. The different profile of the lecture hall can be visibly identified through its half-round shape. The new entrance provides collaborative breakout spaces accessible through an open vertical stair.

The site's adjacency to the San Andreas fault line and the locally extreme temperatures and windy conditions were major influences on the building's placement and orientation. Sustainable features including daylighting and solar screening were included without affecting the construction budget.

3   Entry courtyard

3

San Mateo County Sheriff's Forensic Laboratory and Coroner's Office

San Mateo, California, USA

29,000 square feet / 2,700 square meters
Completion: 2003

The design marries the single-story building's highly technical interior program with the external impact of the sloped site in the San Mateo hills.

Set amid one of California's most picturesque coastal ranges, the site drove the basic design philosophy. An architectural vocabulary consisting primarily of simple planes and common materials maximizes the site's potential without visually competing with it. Low sweeping forms slide effortlessly along the hill and remain hidden from most vantage points. The building orientation maximizes solar energy, natural light, and outside views while minimizing site and contextual impact.

At the same time, this is an assertive building with sharp corners and a dramatically sloped roof. Shifting roof forms fold and intersect with a random balance perfectly suited to the building's hillside setting. Deep overhangs hint at a management strategy for natural light, while generous volumes of glass give the building a light, almost kinetic quality. Sections of mullioned glass are strategically

1

1   North lab bank

2   Rooftop photovoltaics

3   View from west

2

placed to knit the building's various components into a rhythmic whole. Exposed structural elements—especially seismic lateral bracing and inexpensive materials such as split-faced concrete block and aluminum panels—lend the building an unpretentious but sophisticated character.

The stunning visual impact of the building-integrated photovoltaic roof system, which takes on an iridescent purple tone, gives the lab prominence from above the sloping site. The building appears to have been designed as a palette for these solar panels.

3

Sanya Haitang Bay National Seashore
Master Plan

Hainan, China

310 acres / 125 hectares

1   View of bay area seashore

2   Aerial master plan view

Developers on Hainan Island off China's southern coast
are abandoning conventional shoreline resort concepts
in favor of creating a true eco-resort that will capitalize
on the area's virgin beachfronts and organic farming
communities.

The plan embraces the traditional cultural heritage,
allowing for gradual staged redevelopment of the villages
into retirement resorts and assisted-care communities,
as well as training centers in the principal town.

The entire seashore will be developed in a way that
enables the wildlife to flourish as the area becomes self-
sustaining. All products consumed will be grown or grazed
in the immediate vicinity.

1

Sheraton Timika Eco-Hotel

Timika, Irian Jaya, Indonesia

183,000 square feet / 17,000 square meters
Completion: 1994

1   Lobby

2   Exterior pavilion

1

Minimizing the impact of the building on the environment was of primary importance in the design of this remote resort at the edge of a tropical rainforest. The eco-hotel is set amid huge natural gardens at the food of the majestic Puncak Jaya mountain range.

The main lodge rests on a base of local river stone. The supporting stilts elevate guestroom bungalows above the rainforest floor, preserving the fragile nature of the flora, fauna, and water table. An elevated bridge system links to the series of elevated bungalows and a nature trail that meanders throughout the rainforest.

2

3

4

Each bungalow includes 16 guest rooms with screened porches for guests
to enjoy the spectacular natural scenery and more than 90 species of birds.
A palette of regional wood, stone, and textiles, combined with carvings by local
craftspeople, celebrates local resources and traditions.

3   Pavilion at dusk

4   Guesthouse

SJ Berwin LLP Offices

London, UK

200,000 square feet / 20,440 square meters
Completion: 2006

1   Circulation

SJ Berwin consolidated its three separate London offices into the 10 Queen Street Place building. The design aspires to mirror the aesthetics and amenities of a boutique hotel while also revealing the internal workings of the practice to clients. The open-plan law offices promote collaborative work among practice groups. Prime perimeter areas offering views of the Thames River or St. Paul's Cathedral are reserved as generously appointed public breakout spaces. Private offices are fronted by cellular glass.

1

3

4

2

5

2　Interior atrium

3　Reception

4　Break area

5　Balconies along atrium

6

6　Meeting room

7　Stair

Three atria were created to bring additional light and life to the space. The central lift atria provides a vertical artery with the opportunity to see lawyers and colleagues at work in their glass-fronted offices. This is supplemented by the two new atria, which each contain helical stairs of considerable architectural beauty that provide interest and fascination to these areas but also a rapid means of access between floors.

In addition to providing SJ Berwin with an innovative office environment within the large, 50,000-square-foot (4,645-square-meter) floor plate, the project included designing the landlord and tenant receptions, client meeting and entertainment facilities, a café, special deli facilities, and exterior landscaping for a new river-facing roof terrace.

Symantec Executive Boardroom

Cupertino, California, USA

3,300 square feet / 305 square meters
Completion: 2005

1   Boardroom

Form blends with function in Symantec's new executive boardroom. Up to 36 participants can be seated around the 17- by 40-foot (5- by 12-meter) custom-built, high-tech conference table.

Built-in banquette seating on the perimeter allows for informal breakouts and additional seating. A kitchen prep area is separated by a skyfold partition. A private office adjacent to the main room allows the president's assistant to monitor the meeting undisturbed. A smaller conference room also adjoins the boardroom for direct and secure access. A large projection room houses equipment for two 60- by 90-inch (150- by 230-centimeter) rear projection screens and provides high-quality audiovisual presentations and videoconferencing.

1

Time Inc. Conference Center

New York, New York, USA

20,000 square feet / 1,860 square meters
Completion: 2003

The design upgrades Time Inc.'s conference facilities within the landmark Time & Life Building in Manhattan, providing an appropriate, secure setting for important meetings and entertainment events.

The challenge was to provide a variety of spaces that could be used singly or in various combinations. With a variety of flexible meeting spaces and venues, the dozen conference areas range from a small meeting room for eight to a space capable of comfortably seating 150 people. The spaces also had to provide security and privacy for noteworthy and celebrity guests.

1

1   Breakout area
2   Photo collection

4

The design reflects the character of the historic building. Finishes express elegance and durability, and the furniture is comfortable for high-level visitors yet easily adaptable to changing functions.

An archived collection of photographs and other Time Inc. memorabilia reminds visitors of the rich history of the company—the world's largest magazine publisher.

3   Concierge/breakout area

4   Private dining area

3

Tokyo Telecom Center

Tokyo, Japan

1.7 million square feet / 158,000 square meters
Completion: 1995
Associate architect: Nissoken Architects and Engineers

1 Building section

2 Building exterior

Built on reclaimed land at the edge of Tokyo Bay, Tokyo Telecom Center is the axial focus of the area's telecommunications industry. The twin 24-story complex is designed as an abstract form, creating a cube of space within a cube of glass. The two towers are connected at the top by an observation bridge that houses a functional satellite antenna platform. A five-story atrium connects the towers at ground level.

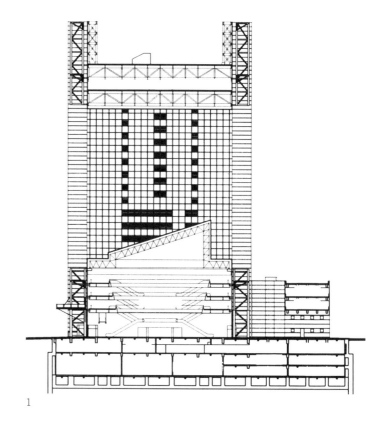

1

4

The curtain wall is composed of nested grids. Inside, a cylindrical skylight supported by latticework draws daylight into the cubic atrium. These themes are integrated throughout the building: cube within cube, squares within squares, and circles within squares.

3　Façade and latticework detail

4　Main entry

3

Tyson Foods
Discovery Center

Springdale, Arkansas, USA

100,000 square feet / 9,290 square meters
Completion: 2007

1   Front entry to research center

Tyson Foods' Discovery Center is a research, development, and training facility designed to transform the company's processes for creating new foods and to bring them to market more quickly.

The center is composed of three interconnected elements: a four-story office building, a product development kitchen building, and a pilot plant. It consolidates the company's food science and culinary professionals and includes 19 test kitchens, a FDA-certified pilot plant, packaging innovation and sensory labs, offices, and a conference and training facility. The kitchens and labs are at the perimeter, with flexible open offices in the middle encouraging collaboration between Tyson's R&D, marketing, and management teams.

2

3

2   Courtyard

3   Connecting "street"

The center's design changes people's perceptions about the existing campus, which is mostly made up of 1970s-era, brown-brick buildings. The simple but modern materials palette includes glass and aluminum, burnt orange Trespa panels that complement and enhance the brown brick, and energy-efficient CENTRIA metal panels.

University Health Network Toronto Hospital New Clinical Services Building

Toronto, Ontario, Canada

800,000 square feet / 74,000 square meters
Completion: 2003

The Clinical Services Building set new standards in state-of-the-art imaging, surgery, and high-acuity patient care in a technologically advanced but healing environment. The design resolves a range of planning issues related to effective health care delivery on an extremely dense urban site adjacent to University Avenue, Toronto's main civic boulevard.

The new 224 bed facility greatly expands the hospital's surgical and imaging capacity. Operating rooms with intraoperative imaging capabilities enable treatment of a variety of complex surgical interventions. A four-story, atrium-like patient court provides a year-round refuge for families, patients, and staff while serving as a beacon to the community.

1   Exterior night

2   Patient court

1

1

The University of Houston-Clear Lake Student Services Building

Clear Lake, Texas, USA

160,000 square feet / 14,865 square meters
Completion: 2005

1   Courtyard

2   East side

The design of the new Student Services Building, the first new building on the campus in 25 years, brings continuity to the campus in terms of form and materials while establishing a fresh typology that sets the stage for the university's next generation of buildings.

The program is divided into two parts, housed within a traditional box-like classroom building that combines dark-bronze metal with precast concrete panels and a more fluid, modern student services building. The three-story glass atrium that links the two buildings serves as a circulation node and provides transparency for future expansion.

2

U.S. Department of State Nairobi Embassy Compound

Nairobi, Kenya

228,000 square feet / 21,180 square meters
Completion: 2005

1

1   Porch

2   Entry canopy

The design was primarily influenced by the political, aesthetic, and security conditions required by the Department of State. The design criteria required that the facility incorporate highly secure, traditional architecture and locally sensitive building materials and provide an image fitting for the United States' representation in a foreign country. This was accomplished by implementing three elements: a porch element, outdoor gathering spaces, and a consular section entrance.

HOK was challenged to establish a compromise between the client's goals of high security and the desire to convey a sense of openness and welcome to the people of Kenya. One common approach to creating a sense of openness is to incorporate a high ratio of exterior glass. Because high glass ratios may pose a security risk for building visitors and occupants, this was ruled out as a solution. The designers found inspiration from many of the classic archetypes of open, welcoming American architecture including the White House and George Washington's mansion at Mount Vernon. The façades of each of these facilities use less than 15 percent exterior glass while extending an additional architectural element that has come to symbolize an American sense of welcome: the porch. The porch element ties into a monolithic stone wall, compositionally focusing attention to the building's main entrance.

Particular attention was given to outdoor spaces within the complex, which, based on the locally temperate climate, can be used throughout the year. The designers drew inspiration from the widespread Kenyan cultural phenomenon of private outdoor "rooms." These outdoor spaces include an amphitheater used for both informal and formal functions. The great lawn is another important outdoor space, serving as an American symbol of arrival. Visiting dignitaries proceed toward the building on the great lawn, which terminates at the porch element. Finally, the courtyard, enclosed by the composition of the buildings on the site, provides an additional outdoor gathering space for staff and visitors to enjoy.

Designed as part of a design/build team with JA Jones International.

3

4

3   Fenestration detail

4   Site detail

5   View of building from memorial plaza

The plaque reads:

JULIAN BARTLEY MEMORIAL PLAZA

THIS PLAZA IS DEDICATED TO THE MEMORY
OF THE FORTY-SIX MEMBERS OF THE
EMBASSY OF THE UNITED STATES OF AMERICA
WHO LOST THEIR LIVES IN THE TERRORIST ATTACK
OF AUGUST 7, 1998

5

U.S. Department of State New Office Building

Moscow, Russia

220,000 square feet / 20,440 square meters
Completion: 2000

2

1 West façade

2 Fenestration detail

This building breaks out of the visual confines of the
State Department compound in Moscow while adding a
contemporary landmark to the skyline. The strong forms
mediate existing site geometries and orient the building
westward to overlook a major urban thoroughfare and park.

3

4

3   Façade detail

4   West façade in skyline

The west façade receives formal attention as the building's face to the city of Moscow. A sweeping, curved curtain wall inserted into the stone-sheathed façade opens onto the outlying panorama. This glass window wall creates shimmering, dynamic images that shift with the natural light and weather conditions.

5

5   Glass stair

6   Elevator lobby

6

U.S. EPA Environmental Research Center

Research Triangle Park, North Carolina, USA

1.2 million square feet / 111,500 square meters
Completion: 2001

1

The Environmental Protection Agency's campus houses more than 2,000 people
and one of the world's largest multidisciplinary groups of environmental scientists.

Building this new research campus presented the agency with an extraordinary opportunity to demonstrate its environmental ethics. The design embodies the EPA's goals for preserving the natural environment, reducing energy use, conserving resources, preventing pollution, and fostering education about sustainable design.

Strategies for energy efficiency and water conservation are saving the EPA $2 million a year in operating costs. Since it opened, the center has become a widely recognized model for sustainability.

1   View from lake

2   Laboratory façade

2

4

The site, which had once been farmland, was densely covered with second-growth hardwoods and conifers. At the high point of the site, a wooded knoll is home to the site's oldest trees; at the low point, a series of small wetlands fronts a man-made lake. Distinct ridges and valleys mark the 60-foot (18-meter) drop to the lake's edge.

3   Stair

4   Atrium

5   Plaza leading to main entrance

6   Model of site plan

5

The design embeds the new campus into the rolling terrain, allowing large portions of the landscape to remain intact. Parking garages built into the hillside reduce the need for surface parking. The campus buildings—four five-story laboratory blocks, three office blocks of three stories, and a centrally located six-story office building—are linked by a series of enclosed atrium spaces that provide a main street of circulation for the complex.

The laboratories' built-in flexibility enables the EPA to keep pace with the constant changes in environmental science. Standard lab modules are paired with a flexible zone that accommodates lab or office use.

6

1

USAA Phoenix Norterra Campus

Phoenix, Arizona, USA

650,000 square feet / 60,387 square meters
Completion: 2000

1   Lobby reception area

2   West terrace

This LEED-certified building responds to Phoenix's unique climate and desert environment. Overall, the building integrates with the land while conserving energy and water, meeting the needs of its occupants, and delivering long-term value by providing a highly productive work environment.

The three-story campus solution consists of a series of low-rise, interconnected office modules organized around an east–west spine. Each module represents an open plan of approximately 35,000 square feet per floor that could be paired with another module to provide as much as 70,000 square feet of flexible space. Limiting building height to a three-floor maximum achieves easy vertical circulation for employees and a building form that integrates visually with the land.

2

3

The contextual design, representative of the surrounding native Sonoran desert, includes a palette of natural Arizona sandstone and copper-colored metal panels contrasting with clear glass. Large ribbon windows banded with copper panels face north and south, incorporating distinctive vertical and horizontal shading devices. These windows are designed to shelter the interior from harsh light while harvesting light deep into the building's footprints. East and west façades are clad in sandstone with smaller punched window openings.

Interior design by Gensler.

3   West façade

4   North façade detail

5   Blue Sky cafeteria

4

5

Warner Music Canada Headquarters

Markham, Ontario, Canada

25,000 square feet / 2,320 square meters
Completion: 2004

1

1   Boardroom

2   Reception area

Warner Music Canada wanted a hip, forward-looking environment for its new head office on the ground floor of a former technology campus outside Toronto.

In the reception area, clean lines and crisp forms convey a sense of professionalism. A long oak desk with a brushed stainless-steel counter rests atop polished, tinted concrete flooring.

The design balances the contrasting needs of "heads-down" business teams and "volume-up" music promotion teams. Pulling offices and workstations away from the perimeter creates a primary circulation path along the nearly full-height windows, which draw in natural light.

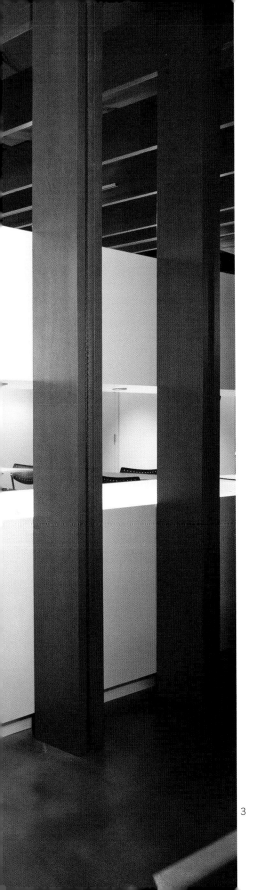

4

Flooring in work zones changes from concrete to neutral
carpeting with a linear pattern, and the ceiling is dropped
for acoustical reasons. Each group is clustered within
a distinct work neighborhood connected to a central,
multipurpose community square. The square encourages
interaction among the two groups, their customers, and
the artists.

Raw materials, dramatic lighting, and oversized images
of Warner's artists infuse the space with energy and give
it a performance feel.

3   Employee lounge

4   Interactive corridor

3

1

William Rainey Harper College Avanté Center

Palatine, Illinois, USA

288,000 square feet / 26,760 square meters
Completion: 2004

1   East entry

2   Site plan

The design integrates more than a dozen educational programs into a single building that establishes a new benchmark for academic excellence, student collaboration, and environmental stewardship. The building functions as an inviting new campus gateway.

As the first project of a phased campus master plan, the design provides a unique solution to a complex building program and creates a benchmark for future campus development. Though it was originally conceived as three separate building programs, it was determined that a combined single building offered economic efficiencies and a unique environment to promote student and faculty interaction. A 600-foot-long (183-meter) multi-story

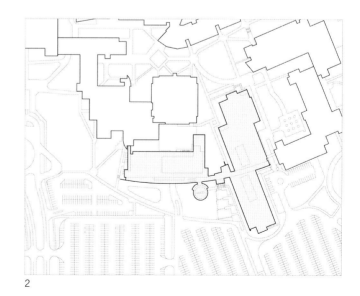

2

3

concourse acts as a linear hub and houses a variety of open student spaces, conference rooms, cafés, and other amenities in addition to connecting to existing academic buildings.

Functionally and visually, the project reflects the client's progressive vision of moving the two-year community college forward by providing students with state-of-the-art facilities that rival or surpass those of neighboring four-year colleges and universities. As an integral part of its community, the building includes flexible lab and teaching spaces to accommodate targeted learning programs in cooperation with its high-technology corporate neighbors and a dental clinic that offers services to the community. Faculty offices are located along major departmental circulation paths in close proximity to classroom and lab space.

The sustainable design strategies include the ventilated exterior cladding system of phenolic resin wall panels that enclose the classroom wings. These environmentally friendly panels are composed of wood fibers from replenishable sources impregnated with phenolic resin incorporating recycled chemicals derived as a byproduct of other manufacturing processes.

WilTel Technology Center Headquarters

Tulsa, Oklahoma, USA

750,000 square feet / 70,000 square meters
Completion: 2002

1   Night exterior

2   Solar well detail

This 15-story "vertical campus" covers one city block in downtown Tulsa, engaging the city while serving as a highly visible landmark.

The 52,000-square-foot (4,830-square-meter) floor plates are connected to a "solar well" vertical circulation core that improves energy efficiency and provides interaction space on balconies and stairways. Each floor functions as a mini-campus, with a library for quiet work, a commons area, a post office and copy center, and a café.

The steel-framed building is essentially transparent from every side. The high-performance curtain wall system features low-emissive fritted glass walls. Glazing at the operating floors is coated with a graduated, ceramic frit that allows maximum daylighting while limiting heat gain and glare and diffusing natural light in office areas.

2

3 Ramp to presentation theater

4 Solar well

3

This graduated pattern blocks high sky brightness while providing clear city views in lower brightness areas. Traditional glazing systems require 50 percent more cooling than this curtain wall.

The 16-foot (5-meter) floor-to-floor heights and sloping ceilings draw daylighting deep into the building core—there are no enclosed perimeter offices to block the natural light. Artificial light is provided by photostatically controlled indirect fixtures that require less energy and produce less heat than traditional lighting.

4

Winrock International Headquarters

Little Rock, Arkansas, USA

24,000 square feet / 2,230 square meters
Completion: 2004

1   Marina view

2   North elevation

1

Winrock International's new headquarters is Arkansas'
first office building to earn a LEED Gold rating. Reflecting
Winrock's mission of promoting sustainable development,
the building serves as a model for environmentally
responsible, affordable construction. The economical design
creates a model that can be easily replicated throughout
Arkansas and the Mississippi River Delta region.

The design concept is for the "post-industrial loft,"
a place where knowledge workers interact to create
innovative solutions. The industrial aesthetic minimizes
the amount of materials used.

The building design is reminiscent of the "dogtrot" house
with a breezeway connecting the main structure to a

2

3   Breezeway

4   Interior

4

smaller conference area and more offices. The two buildings share an on-grade, reinforced concrete porch and are also linked by a second-floor bridge. This design allows air to move between the two buildings, and the ample roof overhang provides cooling shade. The sweeping wing-shaped roof catches rainwater and directs it to an outside cistern where it collects for exterior use. A coating on the metal roof reflects solar energy, reducing heat absorption.

Below the wing-like roof form, the building appears transparent, with tall, floor-to-ceiling windows admitting natural light and waterfront views that enhance the interior workspace. Expanses of glass and skylights are the primary sources for ambient interior lighting and provide a view of the Arkansas River. The interior is appropriately shaded from direct radiation by the overhanging roof and mini-blinds. Interior lights are controlled by a time clock.

Zayed University

Dubai, United Arab Emirates

1.8 million square feet / 168,000 square meters
Completion: 2006

1   Entrance façade

2   Main entrance

HOK, in association with Shankland Cox of the United
Arab Emirates, was selected as part of an international
competition to provide design and construction services
for Zayed University's new campus in Dubai.

The campus is designed to accommodate
approximately 15,000 students in areas of study that
include arts and sciences, business management,
home sciences, telecommunications, and information
technology. The campus features various amenities
including administration buildings, a gymnasium,
an Olympic-size swimming pool, a multipurpose hall,
a cafeteria, and a parking lot.

Located south of Dubai's urban center, the campus is
situated in a hot and humid location that receives little

1

2

3

4

rainfall. The site creates an oasis that gives relief through the use of three types of spaces: the formal central courtyard, the atrium gathering place, and a series of intimate courtyard gardens.

The campus is organized around a central north–south courtyard, which is the main outdoor gathering space. The adjacent Learning Commons central atrium is also used as a gathering space when the outside spaces are too hot. The "commons" is air conditioned with "spill" air from the college wings, reducing excessive air conditioning loads while providing a pleasant temperate environment.

The entrances to all the other academic colleges radiate around the atrium and courtyard, effectively separating the more private classroom and laboratory areas from the university's public area and Learning Commons. Located between classroom wings, the intimate garden courtyards provide an informal gathering place for students and faculty. Each courtyard is given a distinct personality through the use of plantings and paving patterns that differentiate the various academic wings. These courtyard spaces incorporate natural light and water features, and provide students and staff with a variety of outdoor views as they walk between classes.

3   Building façade

4   Learning commons

5   Model of site plan

5

6

7

The overriding character of the university is modern and progressive, expressing the university's commitment to new technology. Yet the design also takes a cue from regional Islamic architecture. Small punched window openings in the massive façades that face out from the internal courtyards echo the mud-brick architecture of some of the region's earliest domestic buildings and historic forts. The design addresses the challenges of the Dubai climate through features like the lightweight tensile structures with Teflon-coated canvas, which provide solar protection to the glass façades and filter natural light. Most campus buildings have flat concrete roofs, exterior insulation, and light-colored ballast to reflect light and heat. These flat roofscapes serve as a contrast to the elliptical light tower and tensile structure above the atrium. As the most outwardly visible elements of the campus, these sculptural roof forms serve as beacons from a distance. At night, uplighting of the light tower and tensile structure adds to their drama and scale.

6   Tower stair rendering

7   Light tower section

8   Ceiling view in tower

1

Zentrum Tower

Mexico City, Mexico

296,000 square feet / 27,500 square meters
Completion: 2002

2

1 Side entrance view

2 Exterior lobby view

The 22-story Zentrum Tower is located in the fast-growing Santa Fe Business district on the eastern edge of Mexico City. Surrounded by mountains and volcanoes, the development is built atop old strip mines.

The tower is a simple but dramatic glass massing that resolves three regular intersecting geometries: a cylinder, a rotated square, and a regular square. The cylinder and the rotated square make up the bulk of the usable space, while the non-rotated square is the service core. The cylinder has a rooftop terrace for the penthouse floor.

The plan's simple, efficient geometry takes advantage of views to the mountains and volcanoes beyond. A rear core scheme responds to both the small plate size and the fact that future residential towers will block existing views. The rotated square increases the frontage of unobstructed views to the north.

3   Main entrance lobby

3

Firm Credits

Executive Committee

Clark Davis
Managing Principal

Tom Robson
Executive

Patrick MacLeamy
Chief Executive Officer

Bob Pratzel
Chief Financial Officer

Bill Hellmuth
President, HOK Inc.

William Valentine
Chairman, HOK Group

Susan Mitchell-Ketzes
Chief Talent Officer

HOK Board of Directors

2008–2009

Susan Grossinger
Senior Vice President
Director of Interior Design,
HOK Los Angeles

Bill Hellmuth
Executive
President, HOK Inc.

Karen League
Senior Vice President
Director of Interior Design,
HOK Atlanta

Patrick MacLeamy
Executive
Chief Executive Officer

Larry Malcic
Senior Vice President
Director of Design,
HOK London

Lui Mancinelli
Senior Vice President
Managing Principal,
HOK Canada

Riccardo Mascia
Senior Vice President
Managing Principal,
HOK Los Angeles

Chuck Siconolfi
Senior Principal
Health Care Director,
New York

Sam Spata
Senior Vice President
Director, buildingSMART

Bill Stinger
Senior Principal
Director of Marketing,
HOK Washington D.C.

William Valentine
Executive
Chairman, HOK Group

Juan Andres Vergara
Vice President
Managing Principal,
HOK Mexico City

David Whiteman
Senior Vice President
Director, Corporate Accounts

Paul Woolford
Senior Vice President
Director of Design,
HOK San Francisco

395

Design Leaders

David A. Amalong, ASLA, RLA
Director of Planning, HOK Denver

With a broad range of international project experience, Mr. Amalong's capabilities range from large-scale master planning to detailed design and implementation. His projects include the Federal Reserve Bank of Minneapolis, Chouteau Lake Master Plan in St. Louis, Sun Microsystems Colorado Campus in Broomfield, Colorado, and the Mary Ann Cofrin Hall Lenfestey Courtyard at the University of Wisconsin – Green Bay.

Annie Bergeron, ARIDO
Design Leader, HOK Toronto

Alternative workplace solutions are the specialty of Ms. Bergeron, who brings specialized knowledge and passion to the design of space. Her experience includes the design of Alliance Films offices, Blake, Cassels & Graydon LLP Offices, MediaCom offices, and the Centre for Health and Safety Innovation.

Erik Andersen, AIA
Lead Designer, Health Care, HOK Chicago

Mr. Andersen works closely with clients to synthesize complex design, planning, and programmatic needs into successful completed projects. His design portfolio includes New York Presbyterian Hospital–Cornell University Medical Center, Northwestern Memorial Hospital Facility Consolidation, and The Ohio State University Medical Center Cancer and Critical Care Tower.

Bob Blaha
Interiors Design Director, HOK St. Louis

With an extensive design portfolio, Mr. Blaha's expertise includes major corporate, government and higher educational projects. His work includes the Boeing Leadership Center, WilTel Technology Center, JWT headquarters, Federal Reserve Bank of Minneapolis, Kellogg headquarters, and British Petroleum headquarters.

Daniela Barbon, ARIDO
Senior Design Leader – Hospitality & Retail Interiors, HOK Toronto

Ms. Barbon has extensive experience in the design and development of high-profile, award-winning projects, with an expertise in brand synthesis. Her projects include the Doha City Centre (Merweb Hotel, Rotana Hotel, and Shangri La Hotel) in Doha, Qatar; Nortel headquarters; Labatt head office; and Centre for Health and Safety Innovation.

Alan Bright, AIA
Senior Project Designer, HOK San Francisco

Mr. Bright's award-winning design portfolio includes public, corporate and commercial, hospitality, justice, healthcare, science and technology, aviation, and mixed-use facilities throughout the U.S., Asia, and Europe. His projects include the Sendai International Airport, San Mateo County Forensics Lab, Phoenix Municipal Courthouse, and State of California Franchise Tax Board.

Henry Chao
Health Care Design Leader, HOK New York

With extensive healthcare design and planning experience, Mr. Chao's design philosophy integrates complex program requirements and constraints into a design that is tailored to the needs and culture of his clients. His current project experience includes the SUNY Downstate Medical Center, University Medical Center at Princeton, and The Ohio State University Medical Center.

Jeffrey S. Davis, ASLA
Senior Landscape Architect,
The HOK Planning Group, St. Louis

Mr. Davis leads multidisciplinary teams through the design, project management, and delivery of projects worldwide. His portfolio includes the King Abdullah University of Science and Technology in Saudi Arabia, BMW North America campus master plan in New Jersey; Brigade Gateway Urban District master plan in India, Dubai Marina in the United Arab Emirates, and Mahindra World City master plan in India.

David Chason, IIDA
Interiors Director, HOK Florida

Mr. Chason's expertise includes corporate, residential and retail interior architecture projects. His experience includes the design of a Latin American headquarters for MTV, HBO and Sony Music; the MasterCard International headquarters, Prime Meridian office tower, Miami-Dade County Children's Courthouse, and the University of Central Florida Burnett College of Biomedical Science Building.

Kenneth Drucker, FAIA
Design Director, HOK New York

During his HOK career, Mr. Drucker has directed the design of many of the firm's most recent benchmark projects. His diverse, high-profile corporate and institutional project work has included Canon USA headquarters, BMW North American headquarters, Winrock International headquarters, the Toronto Hospital, and St. George Intermodal Terminal and Cultural Center.

Ernest Cirangle, AIA
Design Director, HOK Los Angeles

Mr. Cirangle's HOK tenure has included design leadership positions at offices in Los Angeles, Hong Kong, and San Francisco. With expertise in commercial, residential, and mixed-use development, his projects include the LAC + USC Hospital, JTC Summit office tower, Sendai International Airport terminal building, and Tokyo Telecom Center.

Rick Focke
Interiors Design Director, HOK New York

Since joining HOK, Mr. Focke has led the design of numerous large-scale corporate and fashion industry projects. His work includes the AT&T Network Operations Center, Time Inc. headquarters, Ann Taylor headquarters, and the China Life Insurance headquarters in Beijing.

Tony Garrett, IIDA
Interiors Design Director, HOK San Francisco

Mr. Garrett has diverse experience in all aspects of interior architecture. He has served as project designer on high-profile projects for IBM, Cisco Systems, the Clorox Company, JP Morgan Chase, the National Oceanic and Atmospheric Administration, and Caltrans District 4. He also has worked with several furniture manufacturers in the research and development of new furniture products.

Catherine Haley
Interiors Director, HOK Washington, D.C.

Ms. Haley joined HOK in 2008 with extensive corporate and legal project experience. She has received awards for her project work with the US Census Bureau, Pritzker and Hyatt Headquarters, and the Human Rights Campaign.

Colin D. Greene, CNU, APA
Urban Designer, The HOK Planning Group, Washington, D.C.

A co-founder of HOK's New Urban Studio, Mr. Greene is a strong advocate of sustainable development, smart growth, and traditional urbanism. He has designed new communities and neighborhood developments throughout the U.S., including the H Street NE Revitalization Plan in Washington, D.C., Biscayne Boulevard and Brickell Village Public Realm and Urban Guidelines for the City of Miami, and similar studies for Arlington County, Virginia and the D.C. Office of Planning.

Bill Halter, AIA
Design Director, HOK Atlanta

Mr. Halter has expertise in the design of corporate and commercial offices, public and institutional facilities, and mixed-use and retail facilities. His most recent work includes Riverwood 200, Emory University Psychology Building, Carrie Steele-Pitts Life Learning Center, Turner Entertainment Headquarters, and Saint Joseph's Hospital doctor's office building and mixed-use development.

Todd Halamka, AIA
Design Director, HOK Chicago

Mr. Halamka has directed interdisciplinary project teams for the master planning and design of higher education, science and technology, corporate, commercial, public and hospitality projects. His recent work includes the James J. Stukel Towers and UIC Forum at the University of Illinois, Chicago River North Marriott and Clark & Grand Hotel projects in downtown Chicago, and the University of Wisconsin Interdisciplinary Research Complex.

Bill Hellmuth, AIA
President, HOK Inc., and Design Director, Washington, D.C.

A commitment to design excellence by Mr. Hellmuth is demonstrated by his repeated selection for major landmark projects, commercial and federal government facilities, and agency headquarters. His designs include the National Air & Space Museum Steven F. Udvar-Hazy Center, the U.S. Department of State New Office Building in Moscow, the Sheraton Timika Eco-Hotel in Irian Jaya, Indonesia, and Crystal Tower in Kuwait City.

Steven Janeway, AIA
Design Director, HOK Dallas

Since joining HOK, Mr. Janeway has led the design of regional and global corporate, hospitality, mixed-use, and institutional projects. These include the Omni Fort Worth Hotel & Condominiums, Samsung Global Engineering Headquarters in Seoul, Korea, Texas Stadium Redevelopment and master plan, Alcatel USA Headquarters, and Desert Kingdom master plan in Dubai.

Gary Lai
Director of Interior Design, Asia Pacific

Mr. Lai leads the Asia Pacific Interior Studio in all phases of design, from inception to completion with a focus on emphasizing sustainability and ensuring design and service excellence. His project experience includes offices, shopping centers, retail stores, residential, five-star resorts, business hotels, and other commercial interior spaces.

Jeff Kaeonil
Design Director, HOK Hong Kong

Mr. Kaeonil has design experience in the U.S. and the Asia-Pacific region. His portfolio ranges from hotels and resorts to large speculative office developments, mixed-use projects, convention facilities, housing, and master plans.

Serene Lee
Interior Design Director, HOK Hong Kong

Ms. Lee leads the interior design team at HOK's Shanghai and Beijing offices and oversees design direction of all interiors projects across China and the Asia-Pacific region. Having worked in the U.S. and across Asia, she develops innovative design concepts that reflect her extensive experience in various cultures.

Hal Kantner
Director, HOK Visual Communications

During his career, Mr. Kantner has specialized in blending visual communications with cultural attributes to create branded architectural experiences. His clients include 3M, Allsteel, Barclays, Buick, CalSTRS, Capital One, Chrysler, Chevron, Gannett, Hines, IBM, Kodak, Eli Lilly and Company, Motorola, Nortel, Symantec, Sysco, USAA, and Volkswagen.

Larry Malcic, AIA
Design Director, HOK London

Mr. Malcic's design approach is informed by vast professional and academic experience in both Europe and America. His design leadership in London has produced a diverse range of award-winning buildings in the UK, continental Europe, the Middle East, and Central Asia, including Barclays World Headquarters at Canary Wharf, 40 Grosvenor Place, Passenger Terminal Amsterdam, and St. Barnabas Church.

Robert Marshall
Director of Planning, The HOK Planning Group, Toronto

With diverse urban planning and urban design experience, Mr. Marshall is responsible for directing projects ranging from site planning and programming for individual architectural projects to large campuses, city scale master plans and regional studies. His planning and design work spans Canada, the U.S. and the Middle East, as well as throughout Europe, India, Malaysia, Vietnam, and Latin America.

Bill Odell, FAIA
Director, HOK Science + Technology

Mr. Odell has designed buildings for some of the largest and most complicated research campuses. A founding member of the U.S. Green Building Council, he contributed to the creation of the LEED® rating system and co-authored the HOK Guidebook to Sustainable Design. His projects include the King Abdullah University of Science and Technology in Saudi Arabia, Federal Reserve Bank in Minneapolis, Sigma-Aldrich Life Science & High Technology Center in St. Louis, and Mary Ann Cofrin Hall at the University of Wisconsin in Green Bay.

Ali Moghaddasi, AIA
Design Director, Special Projects

Mr. Moghaddasi has extensive design experience in aviation, corporate and commercial developments, mixed-use facilities, and hospitality projects. His project work includes the New Doha International Airport in Qatar, several office towers for Samsung in Korea, San Francisco International Airport Boarding Area G, King Abdulaziz International Airport in Saudi Arabia, and Terminal A at Boston's Logan International Airport.

Clay Pendergrast, AIA, IIDA
Interiors Design Director, HOK Los Angeles

Since joining HOK, Mr. Pendergrast's portfolio has included corporate, entertainment, legal, technology and institutional projects. His work includes America Online's regional headquarters in Beverly Hills, Allsteel and Gunlocke Resource Center in Santa Monica, Biogen Idec pharmaceutical campus in San Diego, Accenture corporate offices in Seattle, and the King Abdullah University of Science and Technology in Saudi Arabia.

Gyo Obata, FAIA
Founding Partner

As the design visionary who shaped the firm, Mr. Obata has more than 50 years of experience in the creation and planning of buildings of all types. Consistently following a philosophy of "designing from the inside out," Mr. Obata believes that the final evaluation of any building must be in terms of human values. His project work includes the Priory Chapel in St. Louis, National Air & Space Museum in Washington, D.C., Kellogg Company headquarters in Battle Creek, Michigan, and Community of Christ Headquarters in Independence, Missouri.

Tom Polucci, AIA, IIDA
Interiors Design Director, HOK Chicago

Mr. Polucci's design philosophy is based on a desire to deliver practical, beautiful workplaces that align with the client's operational goals. His projects include the Allsteel and Gunlocke Resource Center in Chicago, WilTel Technology Center in Tulsa, Ogilvy & Mather offices in Chicago, and the Farrell Learning and Teaching Center at Washington University in St. Louis. He has designed product lines for manufacturers including Mannington Mills and Lees Carpet.

Ripley Rasmus, AIA
Design Director, HOK St. Louis

Mr. Rasmus has directed interdisciplinary design teams for the master planning and design of corporate, commercial and public projects throughout the world. His award-winning work includes the Col. H. Weir Cook Terminal at Indianapolis International Airport, Edificio Malecon office tower in Buenos Aires, Argentina, and WilTel Technology Center in Tulsa.

J. Paul Smead, Associate AIA
Interiors Design Director, HOK Houston

With design experience that includes diverse project types, Mr. Smead's portfolio includes the Chevron Regional Campus, King Abdullah University of Science and Technology, Exxon Headquarters, NASA, and BMC Software Executive Briefing Center.

David Rush, NCIDQ
Interiors Design Director, HOK Atlanta

Mr. Rush's portfolio spans the U.S., Europe, and Asia and includes the design of Cisco's global prototype "next generation" engineering work environment, Siemens/Rolm Executive Briefing Center, Knight Ridder media headquarters, and Sun Microsystems flexible field office prototypes.

Roger Soto, AIA
Design Director, HOK Houston

Mr. Soto has served as a project designer on a broad array of project types, including commercial, healthcare, institutional, and residential. His clients include King Abdullah University of Science and Technology in Saudi Arabia, IBM, HP Compaq, USAA, Sysco Foods, Hines, and Chevron Phillips.

Patrick Sloan
Design Director, HOK Beijing

Mr. Sloan has experience across a broad range of project types, including commercial offices, retail centers, hotels and resorts, residential apartments, and cultural facilities.

Gordon Stratford, MRAIC
Design Director, HOK Canada

Mr. Stratford directs HOK's creative vision in Canada. Beyond providing design leadership, he is actively involved in many of the firm's projects as principal-in-charge. Mr. Stratford uses his extensive experience in corporate and high-tech projects for clients such as Nortel, GE Capital, ITS, and Netscape Canada.

Steven Townsend, Associate AIA, AICP
Regional Director, The HOK Planning Group, Asia Pacific

Mr. Townsend leads a team of urban designers and other planning specialists focusing on sustainable development practices and an interdisciplinary approach to the design process. His projects include master plans for the Haitang Bay National Seashore, Kai Tak Archipelago, Pudfong Event City Tang Town Concept, and An Phu Hung Township.

Yann Weymouth, AIA
Design Director, HOK Florida

Mr. Weymouth is renowned for his design of high-end residential, laboratory, corporate, justice, and museum projects. His most recent cultural work includes four museums in Florida: the completed master plan and four-building expansion of the John and Mable Ringling Cultural Center in Sarasota, the St. Petersburg Museum of Fine Arts' Hazel Hough Wing, the Patricia and Philip Frost Art Museum in Miami, and the Salvador Dali Museum in St. Petersburg.

Bill Valentine, FAIA
Chairman, HOK

Mr. Valentine's diverse design portfolio includes projects representing the corporate, education, justice, aviation, and science and technology sectors. Projects include the Biogen Idec campus in San Diego, Natural Science Building at the University of California in Irvine, Nortel campus in Ottawa, Adobe world headquarters in San Jose, Levi's Plaza in San Francisco, Moscone Convention Center in San Francisco, and Phoenix Municipal Courthouse.

Paul Woolford, AIA
Design Director, HOK San Francisco

Since joining HOK, Mr. Woolford's design experience has included civic buildings, corporate and commercial buildings, educational facilities, libraries, research facilities, and hospitals. His projects include the Georgia Archives, the University of Georgia Paul D. Coverdell Building for the Biomedical and Health Sciences Institute, Shelby Hall, the Whitehead Biomedical Research Facility at Emory University, the CalSTRS headquarters in Sacramento, and the Bay Meadows mixed-use development in San Mateo.

Andy Warner Lacey
Vice President, Senior Interior Designer, HOK London

Mr. Warner Lacey serves as an interior designer and space planner, both in the UK and abroad, for major corporate clients. He is responsible for design concept development, presentation, technical detailing, furniture selection, materials coordination, client liaison, design team and contract management. He has been the lead designer on a number of award-winning law firm projects, including SJ Berwin and Reynolds Porter Chamberlain.

Eddie Wu, OALA, CSAL, ASLA
Senior Landscape Architect, The HOK Planning Group, Toronto

Mr. Wu has professional experience working on international, multi-disciplinary landscape and urban planning projects. Recent projects include the mixed-use commercial center of the King Abdullah University of Science and Technology in Saudi Arabia, Navi Mumbai Energy City master plan in India, Doha City Centre expansion of five hotels built on raised podium structure in Qatar, and the Mavaia landscape concept in Bogota, Colombia.

HOK Employees
2008

Ed Abboud
Mohsen Abdolmohammady
Shadab Abdul Karim
Jafar Abdul-Ghani
Basil Abi-Hanna
Reem Abood
Masoomeh Aboonasr-Shiraz
Yousef Abougabal
Deepu Abraham
Mark Abrams
Poppy Abrego
Mohammed Abu Mhanna
Osama Abu-Omar
Amritha Achuthan
Lemuel Acosta
Pamela Adams
David Adams
Martin Adams
Robert Adams
Alex Adarichev
James Addison
Arthur Adeya
Aaron Adler
Gabriella Adorjan
Chris Aeksarun
Trudi Agbowu
Deneen Agnew
John Agnor
Liliana Aguilar
Frances Ahamad
Alex Akerberg
Nora Akerberg
Niem Akhtar
Javed Akhter
Lina Nasrat Al Yammour
Elsye Alam
Eugene Alday
Karla Alderete
John Aldershof
Rudina Aleksi
Audrey Alemao
Aby Alex
Andres Alfaro
Greg Allen
Fariche Alleyne
Karen Allred
Alex Almanza
Carlos Almeida

Rebecca Almira
Vivian Alonso
Saba Alsaady
Analisa Alt
Ann Althoff
Aaron Altman
Alondra Alvarez
Damian Amador
David Amalong
Brian Aman
Jimmy Amichandwala
Sherin Aminossehe
Annu Anand
Vijay Anandanpillai
Puck Anantakunupakorn
Craig Anderchak
Erik Andersen
Marcy Anderson
Mike Anderson
Chris Anderson
David Anderson
Brandon Anderson
John Andrew
Melissa Andrews
Cerina Anggraini
Christopher Ansell
Stephen Anson
Jeremy Anterola
Bissera Antikarova
Cheryl Apenbrink
Arthur Aragon
Javier Araneda
Amanda Arceo
Mariam Arian
Juan Arias
Camilo Arnesto
Todd Arnold
Hugo Arriojas
Valente Arteaga
Christian Aryo
Michelle Asadies
Reza Asadikia
Suellen Asato
Gabriela Ascencio
Sabrina Ash
Ian Ashcraft-Williams
Aileen Asher
Mark Askew

Pat Askew
Orlin Atanassov
Ross Attridge
Dana Aubrey
Kerry Aucamp
Katie Augustine
Tyrone Austin
Dimitri Avdienko
Ruben Aya-Welland
Glenn Aziz
Dhiren Babaria
Tim Baca
Adam Bachtel
Carrie Back
Susan Baerwald
Maribel Baez-Krawczyk
Bob Bahan
Mary Bailey
Edith Bailon
Breck Baird
Nick Bakaysa
Jack Baker
Brooke Ballachey
Jennifer Ballou
Aspram Balyan
Florence Balzat
Jaco Bam
Teena Ban
Natalie Banaszak
Mark Banholzer
Rachel Bannon-Godfrey
Wendy Bantle
Miguel Bao
Dhaval Barbhaya
Daniela Barbon
Derrick Barendse
Ana Baresic
Andrea Bariciak
Ed Bark
Megan Barker
Samantha Barker
Izumi Barkhouse
Matthew Barlow
Libby Barnert
Casey Barnett
Dean Barone
Bob Barr
Andrew Barraclough

Glenroy Barrett
Gerardo Barrientos
Barbara Barrier
Robert Barringer
Crystal Barriscale
Armando Barron
John Bartolomi
Sabine Bartzke
Nancy Basler
Ashley Bass
Giovanna Bassi
Amanda Bassiely
Toby Bath
Kelly Bathe
Christina Batista
Gerrit Baumann
Julio Bautista
Jessamy Baxter
Nicholas Baylis
Yasmeen Bebal
Chris Beck
Susie Becker
Kasia Bednarek
Josh Behrns
Morteza Behrooz
David Beker
Misty Bell
Jennifer Benjamin
Colin Benson
Kris Benson
Robb Berg
Jim Berge
Annie Bergeron
Linda Bernauer
Matthew Bernstine
Joe Berra
Sebrina Berra
Bernadette Berry
James Berry
Todd Bertsch
Claudia Beruldsen
Maria Beslin
Namrata Betigiri
Kelly Betts
Anuj Bhandari
Meenal Bhandari
Chirayu Bhatt
Harish Bhatt

Harpreet Bhons
Jarek Bieda
Alessandro Bigolin
Kelsey Birkett-Bennett
Clarinda Bisceglia
Jennifer Bishop
James Blackadar
Bob Blaha
Tim Blair
Emily Blocher
Elissa Boedeker
Maria Bogdanova
Todd Bogust
Adrienne Bohan
Sean Bolden
David Boles
Nicholas Bonard
Tracy Bond
Simon Bone
John Bone
Hendra Bong
Claudia Bonilla Lopez
Navara Boon-Long
Mark Borchardt
Zach Borders
Elisa Borgese Schneider
Greg Boshart
Ryan Boshoff
Bryant Bosland
Zorana Bosnic
Oza Bouchard
Steven Bourguignon
Stephen Bourne
Michele Bouterse
Mark Bowers
Eric Bowman
Katie Bowman
Abraham Boyd
Nicolas Bracco
Sam Bradley
Jamie Bradshaw
Frederick Braggs
Chuck Brandau
Raphael Brandsma
Stephen Brandt
Cari Bray
Bob Brendle
Clare Brennan

Christopher Brett
Teresa Bridges
Joshua Bridie
Aaron Briggs
Ninah Briggs
Alan Bright
Lauren Brightwell
Jose Briones
Krista Briske
Cathy Britt
Sean Britt
Tony Brocato
Sharon Brodie
Joann Brookes
Stephen Brookover
Laura Brooks
Ken Brooks
Dianne Brown
Ken Brown
Hillary Brown
Cheyne Brown
LeeLee Brown
Sherita Brown
Christopher Brown
Chris Browne
Michael Browning
Duncan Broyd
Jim Bruce
Marissa Bruce
Katharina Brunner
Bruce Brunner
Kaleena Brzozowski
Anna Buchan
Todd Buchanan
Kim Buchanan
Anthony Buchanan
Mia Buchignani
David Buckley
Amanda Buckli
Tony Buckli
Ami Buckner
Barbara Budzinski
Randy Buescher
Leila Bugaoan
Richard Bugbee
Steve Buhler
Sara Bullington
Kimberley Burchart
Gillian Burgis
Kimberly Burke
Tod Burkhead
Bill Burmeister
Emily Burnett
Amanda Burns
Katie Burns
Thomas Burnworth
Barbara Burr
Ida Burrell
Kathy Burstadt
Sharon Burton
Eva Busato

Julia Busby
Steve Butler
Karen Butts
Marisa Caban
Jack Cade
Michelle Cadena
Jessica Cadkin
Karen Cagney
Frankie Cahanin-Rylee
Sarah Cahill
Sheila Cahnman
Andre Calderon
Karen Calfee
Janet Calkins
Ray Call
Alesia Call
Gerald Callo
BickVahn Cam
Robyn Cameron
Heather Cameron
David Camp
Brian Campbell
Robert Campbell
Karen Candies
John Cannon
John Cantrell
Xi Cao
Yuhong Cao
Jessica Cao
Omer Caparti
Albert Capetillo
Jennifer Capson
Antonia Cardone
Jim Cardoza
Lesley Carmona Lewis
Vasile Carnabatu
Nicole Carpenter
Carolyn Carpenter
Brett Carter
Lisa Carter
Natalia Carvajal
Karen Carvalho
Dan Cash
Maxwell Cash
Erika Casillas
Ryan Casse
Mark Cassimus
Juan Castaneda
Levy Castaneda
Rose Castillo
Suong Castillo
Vince Catalli
Marilyn Catinella
Lacey Causseaux
Frank Cauthen
Danielle Caylor
Jennifer Cayton
Rebecca Ceballos
Henry Cedillo
David Cerniglia
Victoria Cervantes

Gabriel Cervantes
Patricia Cervantes
Angelica Chacon
Pep Si Chai
Jet Chai
John Champer
Rhoda Chan
Vicky Chan
Catherine Chan
Edward Chan
Jen-Shen Chan
Benjamin Chan
Sau-Mui (Jane) Chan
Sammy Chan
Patsy Chan
Jerry Chan
Krit Chandrema
Kathy Chaney
Carlos Chanez
Emily Chang
Steven Chang
TH Chang
Huan-Chou Chang
Mike (Li-Chung) Chang
Henry Chao
Adele Chapin
Richard Chapman
Mohamed Charkas
John Charters
Philip Chase
David Chason
David Chassin
Shoma Chatterjee
Yamelin Chavez
John Cheek
Hunvey Chen
Katherine Chen
Judy Chen
Ruby Chen
Ting Chen
Rosa Cheney
Yvonne Cheng
Chelsea Cheng
Jeffrey Cheng
Samson Cheng
Albert Cheng
Ka For (Bob) Cheng
Helen Cheuk
Kerry Cheung
Fan Cheung
Chi-Kit Cheung
Doug Chew
Robert Chicas
Jose Chieng
Andrew Childs
Sandy Chin
Ting Chin
Jack Chin
Porfirio Chirino
Alice Chiu
Anna Chlad

Frank Chlad
Miroslaw Chmuro
Jacalyn Chnowski
Soo Mi Choi
Hack Jong Choi
Moon Choi
Rahul Chopra
Andy Chow
David Chow
Jackie Chow
Alexandra Chow
Teng Chow
Darren Chow
Zach Christeson
Peggy Chu
Terry Chu
Randy Chubb
Eun Chung
Jonathan Chung
Eve Chung
Christine Chung
Jeff Churchill
Weronika Cichosz
Barbara Ciesla
Julio Cifuentes
Eungee Cinn
Daniela Ciolac
Ernest Cirangle
Isilay Civan
Karan Clark
Monique Clark
Nathan Clark
Brian Clark
Lisa Clark
Derrek Clarke
Wendy Cleggett
Kerry Clifford
Lisa Clifton
Shaun Clopton
Gordon Cobban
Owen Cockle
Sanjeev Coelho
David Coghill
Jeff Cogliati
Jon Cohen
Claire Cohen
Sandra Colavecchia
Donna Colbourn
Stacey Coleman
Leesa Coller
Mickey Collins
Paul Collins
Lalyn Collure
Christopher Colosimo
Bill Connor
Brian Cook
David Cook
Gregory Cook
Michael Cook
Neil Cooke
Alex Cooke

Karetha Cooper
Richard Corbeil
Fernando Cordero
Maryann Cornejo
John Corson
Jason Corson
Francesco Cortese
Moira Coughlan
Kristin Couris
Adam Cox
Sean Cox
Robert Cox
Nicole Crabiel
Steven Crang
Ben Crawford
Chip Crawford
Carolina Creciente
Donald Cremers
Gary Creson
Lisa Cresswell
Don Crichton
Rex Criswell
Barb Cronn
Brad Crown
Annie Crumbaugh
Piedad Cruz
Gonzalo Cruz
Jorge Cruz
Ivy Cruz
Wayne Cully
Maja Cunningham
Matthew Cunnington
Taylor Currell
Zach Curtman
David Cutmore
Brent Cutshall
Mike Cutulle
Jay Dacon
Morgan Daenzer
Emily Dai
Neshaminy Dalal
Susan Dame
Hui Dang
Joshua Daniel
Kallie Daniel
Keri Daniel
Rocco Danna
Janice Dannebaum
Tom Darmody
Ted Davalos
Graham Davies
Melissa Davis
Clark Davis
Jeff Davis
BJ Davis
Rose Davis-Dunn
Susan Davis-McCarter
Shahrzad Davoudi
Barry Day
Elvira Dayel-Kogan
Tim De Alwis

Helena De Costa	Toni Dooley	Jerry Equi	Susan Finlay	Nikola Gakovic
Darrell de Grandmont	Jose Doormann	Lars Erickson	Jeremy Finnell	Tim Gale
Jolene De Jong	Gena Dorminey	Sean Erickson	Marvis Firmage	Blake Gallagher
Maura De La Cruz	Ellen Doty	WillErwin	Brian Fishenden	Candice Gallinger
Sergio De La Espriella	Simon Douch	Laura Eshelman	Tam Fisher	Francesco Gallo
Amanda De Sanctis	Dana Dougherty	Peter Espe	Norman Fisher	Akshay Gandhi
Carly Debacker	Jim Doussard	Javier Espinoza	Jim Fitzgerald	David Gange
Chris Defosset	Kimberly Dowdell	Ana Espinoza	Cynthia Flamm	Pipat Ganlayanasant
Elizabeth Del Real	Christine Dowdy	Fabricio Esquivel	Marc Flax	Angela Gao
Mark Del Rosario	Lisa Downs	Manuel Esquivel	Ian Fleetwood	Joice Garcia
Dermot Delaney	Arick Doyle	Jun Estrella	Scott Fleming	Michael Garcia
Joseph Delehanty	Jeff Dreesman	Frank Etro	Lauren Flemister	Jonel Garcia
Juan DeLeon	Erin Dreisbach	Kathleen Ettienne	Daniel Fletcher	Jorge Garcia
Pat Delmas	Corinne Drobot	Eulogia Eulopa	David Fletcher	Miguel Garcia
Christine DeLong	Rich Drozd	Jeongsu Eun	David Fletcher	Robert Gardner
Linda Delos Santos	Kenneth Drucker	Whitney Evans	Cassandra Flood	Jon Gardzelewski
Danny DeLuca	Nicole Dudragne	Johnny Evans	Enrique Flores	Pooja Garg
Mike Demma	Jon Duey	Steve Evans	Gil Flores	Mike Garrett
Debbie Dempsey	Nikki Duffner	Ralph Evans	Rick Focke	Tony Garrett
Yi Deng	Leah Duffy	Kim Even	Karen Foley	Angelisa Garrett
Jonathan Derby	Katie Dufresne	Mohamed Eweis	Jek Fong Charles Lee	Michele Garza
Douglas Deremer	Leah Dugan	Jarrett Ewing	Roger Fontaine	Terri Gatlin
Geeta Deshpande	Paul Duggleby	Amy Fabry	Lye Foong	Paula Gaviria
Helen Desjardins	Gilbert Duldulao	Marcela Face	Steve Foran	Andrew Gayer
Brett Desmarais	Genee Dunn	Danilo Failangca	Melissa Force	Ivana Gazic
Guy Despatis	Randy Dunn	Rogelio Failangca	Gillian Foreman	Nancy Gearty
Jan Deweer	Kathie Dunn	Chris Fannin	Corey Forst	Suzy Genzler
Claire Dexter	John Dupuy	Marcelo Farias	Troy Fosler	Ricardo George
Jerry Dezern	Josefina Duran	Alain Farivar	Jonas Foster	Alek Georgiou
Cyrus Dezfuli-Arjomandi	Jessica Duran	Shazia Farooqui	Mike Fowler	Ziba Geramikhosh
Nadine Di Iulio	Carly Durant	Pauline Farrar	Emily Fowlkes	Rony Ghadban
Ed Diamante	Sarah Durio	Jo Farrell	Kathleen Fox	Murad Ghaith
Laura Diamante	Teresa Durkin	David Fassett	Luigi Franceschina	Kiranjit Ghattaora
Ronaldo Diamse	Tamara Dvorsky	Charles Fattore	Catherine Franssen	Michael Ghezzi
Robert Diaz	Jazdia Dwyer	David Faubion	Wyatt Frantom	Lauren Gibbs
Ximena Diaz	Angie Earlywine	Ryan Favier	Bruce Fraser	Gerard Giblin
Judy Diehl	Karen Easter	Don Fedorko	Michelle Fraser	Stephanie Gibson
Jason Diehl	Rona Easton	Cathleen Feland	Cliff Frazee	Sarah Gibson
David Dike	Richard Eastwick	Dallas Felder	Sarah Freeman	Tomasz Gil
Indrawati Dilaila	Timothy Eavis	Kris Feldmann	Kim Frey	Thomas Giles
Saad Dimachkieh	Lois Edford	Senada Feratovic	PamFried	Aman Gill
Chris Dimaisip	Michael Edwards	Alem Ferede	Liz Friedman	Bob Gillcrist
Dinah Dimalanta	Paul Edwards	Denette Fereria	Dan Friedman	Dennis Gillespie
Darlyn Dimayuga	Zuhal Ege	Pat Ferguson	Brandi Frierdich	Jim Gillette
David Dimitry	James Eggleton	Sarah Ferguson	Matthew Friesen	Tony Gillund
Tarik D'Introno	Neil Eisenberger	Abdel Ferhi	Erich Friesen	John Gilmore
Crystal Dippre	John Eisenlau	Mark Fernandes	Andrea Frigolett	Jessica Ginther
Milorad Djukic	Giles Ekins	Ramon Fernandez	Cris Fromboluti	Patrick Gleason
Sanja Djulepa	Patricia Ekins	John Fernandez	Sarah Fronick	Fred Goebel
Isabella D'Nazareth	Mignon Elayda-Fulton	Jincy Fernandez	Edith Fuentes	Christy Goessling
Magdalena Dobranowski	Sayed Elkarmouty	Luis Fernandez De Ortega	Deborah Fuller	Mike Goetz
Adam Doddridge	Bridget Ellgass	Rodolfo Ferranco	Michael Fuller	Tino Golchin
Kathy Doi	Ben Elliott	Kathryn Ferrell	Glenise Fuller	Suzette Goldstein
Beverly Dolson	Christopher Elliott	Aidan Ferriss	Laura Fyles	Emily Golembiewski
Arnel Domingo	Jordan Ellis	Lynn Ferron	Vivian Gabrail	Luba Golyand
Alberto Dominguez	Salwa El-Shabasy	Jim Fetterman	Eilis Gaffney	Javier Gomez
Derek Don	J. C. Elston	Steve Fichet	Stephen Gage	Liseth Gomez
Sarah Donato	Ben Embir	Aaron Fields	Tim Gaidis	Robert Gonzales
Tao Dong	Teresa Endres Cabrera	Miguel Figueroa	Erika Gaies	Chris Gonzalez
Rachel Doniger	David Endsley	Agnes Filar	Dawn Gajewski	Megan Gonzalez
Paul Donnelly	Nellie Enriquez	Lynn Filar	Danka Gakovic	Julio Gonzalez

Margaret Goodin
Martina-Susanne Goodman
Candice Goodwin
Jenny Gora
Anne Gorbutt
Lance Gorbutt
Tawn Gorbutt
Mark Gordon
Robert Gordon
Helen Gorodkin
Paul Gotaco
Michael Gould
Thomas Gould
Jennifer Goulden
Tom Goulden
Naveen Govind
Paula Grad
Michael Graham
Sara Graham
Fotis Grammatikopoulos
Peter Grandine
Tony Granero
Tauwana Grant
Cynthia Grant
Trip Grant
Emily Grant
Rob Gray
Victoria Gray
Anna Gray
Lisa Green
Nicola Greenaway
Colin Greene
Valerie Greer
Tara Gremminger
Kurt Griesbach
John Grieve
Gaute Grindheim
Alvaro Grisales Araoz
Susan Grossinger
Simon Groves
Kanlin Gu
Hector Guayaquil
Shelby Guazzo
Andrei Gubovici
Amber Guenther
Oanh Guerra
Greg Guerra
Geraldine Guevarra
Christele Guibout
Walter Guidry
Christophe Guillot
Rika Gunawan
Lalit Gurjar
Nimrod Gutman
Mario Guttman
Edgar Guzman
Matt Hackbarth
Ihad Haddad
Jesse Hager
Ermias Hagos
Erik Haight

Ermias Haile
Crystal Haines
Daniel Hajjar
Farzine Hakimi
Faezeh Hakimzadeh
Todd Halamka
Catherine Haley
William Hall
Jason Hall
Bill Halter
Shwan Hamed
Terri Hamilton
Jason Hamlin
Ji Hee Han
Steven Handelman
Janice Handiak
Courtney Handlan
Debra Handy
Andrew Haney
Arlene Hanna
Geoffrey Hannington
Sasha Hanoomansingh
Halim Hardan
Jean Hardy
Natalie Harewood
Meive Harford
Steve Hargis
Jan Harmon
Amanda Harnitz
Michael Harris
Suzy Harris-Brandts
Phoebe Hart
Colleen Hart
Dan Hartmann
Brandon Hartz
Tina Haskins
Martin Haskins
Zuhair Hassan
Darren Hastings
Timothy Hatton
Taisha Haymon
Yong He
Marilyn Hecker
Kelly Heet
April Heflich
Chris Heikkila
Helen Heilmeier
Jon Heimdahl
Craig Hein
Peter Heinbecker
Susan Heinking
Stephanie Heit
Michael Heller
Bill Hellmuth
Jared Heming
Scott Hemlock
Susan Henderson
Andrew Henderson
Ricardo Hendi
Kristen Henry
Miranda Hensley

Stephen Herbert
Jacy Herendeen
Maurice Herman
Brenda Hernandez
Gabriel Hernandez
Ken Herold
Brian Herrera
Luis Herrera
Mari Herrington
Daniel Herriott
David Herron
Frank Hersom
Ramona Hess
Julie Hick
Pia Hill
Christopher Hillegas
Daimian Hines
Michele Hines
Tim Hinkle
Jack Hipps
Chloe Hiyu
Chris Hlavinka
Olive Ho
Han His Ho
Steve Ho
Lyle Hodgin
Leah Hofferkamp
Eric Hoffman
Jimm Hoffmann
Kim Hogan
Dana Hogstedt
Eli Hoisington
Megan Holder
Robert Holland
Will Hollingsworth
Lara Hollis
David Hollister
Winston Holloway
Dave Holloway
Michael Holm
Jacqueline Holt
Eliza Honey
Tom Hook
Matt Horvath
Elizabeth Horvitz
Farhad Hosany
Hossam Hosni
Brian Houle
Chris Housley
Randy Houts
Herman Howard
Jonathan Howe
Kandice Hribar
Yat-Mei (May) Hsiang
Carrie Hsu
Cheung (Daniel) Hsueh
Ming Hu
Aeron Huang
Andy Huang
Joanne Huang
Samuel Huang

Susan Huang
Ford Hubbard
Bill Hudgens
Jenna Hudson
Paula Huerta
Susan Hughes
Sue Hughes
Scott Hughes
Barry Hughes
Christina Hui
Keith Hui
Casey Hull
Allen Humphries
Pearl Hung
CE Hunter
Stephanie Hur
Paul Hurley
Anne Hutton
David Huxham
Jenny Hyatt
Mike Hyland
Yuntaek Hyun
Waleed Ibrahim
Michele Idoine
Georgine Ilesco
Nestor Infanzon
Chuck Ingrum
Joe Intriago
Carol Ishii
Cliff Isom
David Ivey
Larry Izegbu
Kristin Jackson
Sherril Jackson
John Jackson
Christian Jacob
Bianca Jagers
Nasreen Jahangeer
Monique Jahn
Stefan Jakobek
Hafeez Jamal
Wynne James
Joseph Jamieson
Steven Janeway
Jim Janssen
Thomas Jarrett
Ashani Jayasinghe
John Jedzinak
Cheryl Jefferies
Jaki Jefferson
Rachael Jekki
Brian Jennett
Justin Jennings
Tamara Jensen
Jeff Jensen
Rosa Maria Jerez
Salem Jiddou
Rebecca Jimenez
Juan Carlos Jimenez
Pavel Jimenez
Rita Jin

Aaron Johansen
Niji John
Leslie Johns
Nicole Johnson
Greg Johnson
Carl Johnson
Matthew Johnson
Tom Johnson
Jeff Johnston
Paul Jolly
Keith Jones
Dale Jones
Regina Jones
Elizabeth Jones
Hilary Jones
Erik Jones
Jascynda Jones
Mike Jones
Janet Jones
Bryan Jones
Phillip Jones
Laura Jones
Kelly Jordan
Sanja Jovanovic
Michael Jrab
Martha Juarez
Carolina Juarez
Pam Juba
May Julsuwan
Anju Jutley
Rachel Kaatmann
Elaine Kabala
Rick Kacenski
Tom Kaczkowski
Jeff Kaeonil
Amad Kafarani
Gundars Kajaks
Hoshiko Kamiya
Drew Kane
Shane Kane
Albert Kaneshiro
Diana Kang
Youn Mi Kang
Byung Kang
Atul Kansara
Gopi Kanth
Allison Kantner
Hal Kantner
Inga Kantor
Cagri Kanver
Edward Kao
Nicky Kaplan
Robert Karamitsos
Bonnie Karampatsos
Sara Kardan
Sari Karki Rajabi
Rajas Karnik
Lu Kasawat
Andrea Kastner
Shimpei Katayama
Thangavel Kathirvel

Sandeep Kathuria
Kevin Katigbak
Jack Kato
Ziad Kattan
Michael Katzin
Hiroyuki Kawakami
Brian Keating
Timeirya Keels
Nicole Kegevic Leighton
Marcy Keiser
Ron Keller
Michael Keller
Jim Kelley
Jim Kellogg
Robert Kellogg
Ashley Kelly
Scott Kelly
Andrew Kelmers
Howen Kelmers
Wayne Kelusky
Patrick Kendall
Angus Kennedy
Mark Kennedy
Jason Kerensky
James Kerrigan
Jim Kessler
Rania Khalil
Tanzil Khan
Samira Khan
Ritesh Khanna
Gaurang Khemka
Maissa'a Khidher
Emmanuelle Khoii
Hady Khorsheed
Ira Khulbe
Andrew Kilmer
Sue Kim
Sun Woo Kim
Young Im Kim
Jeong Heon Kim
Eric Kim
Harry Kim
Jongkouk Kim
Joo Kim
Jung-Ha Kim
GunWoo Kim
Jinkyung Kim
June Kim
Jun Kim
Yee Kim
Ashley Kim
Earl Kincaid
Don King
David King
Jonathan King
Donna Kinsley
Duncan Kirk
James Klaiber
Cordelia Klem
Meredith Klingsporn
Susan Klumpp

Colleen Knapp
Keith Knickerbocker
Craig Knight
Melissa Knight
Thomas Knittel
Gary Knoll
John Knowles
Steve Knudsen
Sarah Kobrinsky
Evelyn Koch
Dorothy Kochanski
Eric Koffler
Annabella Koloskov
Lexi Kolt-Wagner
Ga Jen Kong
Hadi Koo
Ryan Kopp
Lara Koretsky
Chris Korsh
Brett Kostial
Helen Kostuch
Basel Kotob
Jackie Kotz
Vesselin Kovatchev
Yoshi Koyama
Chris Krahn
Olivera Kraincanic
Ryan Kranz
Clare Krause
Katy Krause
Dan Kretchmer
Rebecca Krug
Joanna Kruk
James Krushas
Jacklyn Krusleski
Catherine Kucher
Rahul Kulkarni
Priya Kumar
Prasoon Kumar
Erdim Kumkumoglu
Monika Kumor
Koya Kunhi
Veronica Kunkemueller
Jay Kuo
Joe Kury
Eric Kutche
Frank Kutilek
Gary Kuzma
Ryan Kuzma
Kurl Kwak
Steve Kwok
Koma Kwok
Yu Na Kwon
Amy Kwong
Phillip Kwong
Antonio La Rosa
Robert Labonte
Andy Lacy
Eberhard Laepple
Dennis Laflen
Terry Laflen

Gary Lai
Stephen Laico
Gregory Lake
David Lalush
Joanna Lam
Juliette Lam
Rika Lam
Clarissa Lam
Katia Lambert
Alfredo Landaeta
Freddie Landaverde
Anica Landreneau
Allisa Landry
Cindy Landry
Larry Lane
Raymond Lane
Alison Lang
Shala Lang
Geoffrey Lang
Melanie Laplante
Carlo Laquian
Vale Larson-Brasted
Carolyn Lascelle
Alice Lau
Martin Lau
Jason Lau
Chris Laul
Francisco Laurier
Kathleen Lauth
Karen Laveen
Mark Lavender
Jacqueline Lavigne
Genevieve Lavoie
Amy Law
Melanie Law
Stephen Lawlis
Ben Lawrence
Ethel Lazaro
Mary Ann Lazarus
Jillian Lazzarini
Tuyet Le
Cathy Le
Chonnah Le
Karen League
Stephen Leahy
Megan LeBlanc
Lee Leboeuf
David Leckie
Sang Hee Lee
Carol Lee
Elaine Lee
Do-Hyung Lee
Ju Hyun Lee
Sabina Lee
Seung Lee
Jessica Lee
Yun Ho Lee
Choong Hun Lee
Monling Lee
Ivy Lee
Edith Lee

Kash Lee
Vivian Lee
Christopher Lee
Azaria Lee
Shawn Lee
Serene Lee
Wing-Kit Lee
Stewart Leffler
Sandi Leicht
Carrie Leighton
Daina Leja
Don Lemonds
April Lenkey
Heather Lents
Joanna Leo
Danielle Leon
Alejandro Leonardo Zabala
Barry Leong
Bessie Leong
Anthony Leslie
Sandra Lester
Jean Letherby
Lennox Leung
Tom Leung
Amanda Leung
Josephine Leung
Michael Levendusky
Daniel Levin
Stuart Lewis
Kelli Lewis
Doris Lewis
Robert Lewis
Richard Leyendecker
Hong Li
Jenny Li
Amanda Li
Ricky Li
John Li
Olivia Li
Yue Li
Alana Liane
Leon Liang
Anny Liang
Joyce Liang
Kyle Libersat
Katya Lichtenstein
Pam Light
Maja Likakis
Alistair Lillystone
Erwin Lim
Michael Lim
Watson Lim
Jonathan Lim
Yichen Lin
Laura Linn
Michael Linville
William Liow
Robert Lipson
Marsha Littell
Leigh Ann Little
Kenneth Litwin

Eric Liu
Nicole Liu
Tony Liu
Ocean Liu
Season Liu
Xiaoming Liu
Matt Livermore
Alexandra Llobet
Marion Lloyd
Debbie Lloyd
Yvonne Lo
Paul Lo
Evelyn Lo
Dana Logan
Kyeomishia Logan
Yu Leung Lok
Natalia Lombardi
Joyce Loney-Brenes
Merrill Long
Mark Longree
Santiago Loo
Natalie Lopes
Angela Lopez
Carlos Lopez
William Lopez Campo
Andrew Loreman
Ryan Lorey
Jules Loth
Tiffini Lovelace
Courtney Lovell
Justin Lowe
Joyce Loy
Michael Lu
Ying Lu
Michelle Lucas
Kelvin Lugo
Monica Luk Tsz Ying
Briony Lumb
Scott Lumsden
Sabina Luongo
Jelena Lustica
Charlie Lutz
Tina-Tien Luu
John Lyon
Duncan Lyons
Ann Ma
Steven Ma
Maggie Ma
Udo Maar
Renee Maarse
Diosdado Macapagal
Cara MacArthur
Keith MacDonald
Linda Macias
Howard Mack
Erika Mack
Warren Mack
Neil Mackenzie
Patrick MacLeamy
Domingo Macotela
Todd Macyk

Ana Madariaga
Christof Madeiski
M Madhumitha
Jeanine Madison
Celeste Madrigal
Bruce Madsen
Noriko Maeda
Arrizky Magetsari
Peter Magoulick
Samantha Mah
John Mahon
Cole Major
Tansy Mak
Ho Pong Mak
Ting Shan Mak
Wilson Mak
Renee Mak
Sadie Makarechi
Larry Malcic
Penny Malina
Andy Malkus
Mark Maloy
Lui Mancinelli
Anjali Mangalgiri
Zhanna Manko
Richard Manna
Tom Mannerud
Jennifer Mannier
Andrea Manning
Ryan Manning
Liam Mannion
Randy Mao
Weiss Mar
Matt Maranzana
Jonah Margarella
Franco Marinaro
Olimpia Maritaegui
Lisa Marker
Susan Marney
Michelle Marotta
Cristina Marotto
Ligia Marroquin
Gary Marsh
Robert Marshall
Jennifer Martin
Katie Martin
Jon Martin
Paula Martin
Char Martin
Michael Martin
Jorge Martinez
Cicilia Martinez
Victor Martinez
Mayra Martinez
Alberto Martinez
Carlos Martinez
Juan Martinez
Marco Martinez
Jacquie Martinez
Riccardo Mascia
Thomas Mason

Hanadi Masri
Fiorella Massa
Megan Mast
Paul Matelic
Hagen Materne
Lesley Mathers
Mahshid Matin
Laura Matson
Akiko Matsumoto
Mounia Matta
Terry Mattison
Paula May
Lauren May
Jessica May
Hassan Maynard
Frank Mayo
Robert McAuley
Meghan McBride
Jay McCabe
Ted McCagg
Michael McCallum
Mike McCarty
Catherine McCluan
Scott McCombs
Mac McCoy
Zach McCoy
Ed McCrary
Sara McCullough
Kelly McDonald
Devin McDowall
Melissa McElroy
Roger McFarland
Jennifer McGibbon
Ian McGillivray
Stephen McGrane
John McGuire
Molly McIntyre Hair
Lauren McKenna
Paul McKenzie
Mike McKeown
Erin McLaughlin
Christa McManus
Claire McPoland
Kerri McShea
David Mecham
Jane Medina
Scott Meekins
Mili Mehta
Vic Mehta
Dev Mehta
Ignacio Mejia
Anthony Mekel
Elias Mela
Beate Mellwig
Jacinta Mendes
Shiva Mendez
Sandy Mendler
Armando Meneses
Craig Menn
Foard Meriwether
Melissa Merryweather

Todd Meyer
Juana Meyer
Tyler Meyr
Jesse Michael
Carla Michel
Marie Mihalik
Hayam Mikhail
Michael Milano
Ronda Miles
Nolan Miller
Lee Miller
Ron Miller
Sarah Miller
Kirk Millican
Amanda Millner
Daniel Mills
Kirk Minton
Sava Miokovic
Steve Mirman
Anna Misanvu
Chirag Mistry
Sunil Mistry
Dan Mitchell
William Mitchell
Susan Mitchell-Ketzes
Sonia Mithan
Rahul Mittal
Teruka Miyauchi
Ruthy Mizrahi-Olti
Andrea Moeder
Ali Moghaddasi
Arrash Moghaddasi
Priya Mohan
Nilanjana Mohanram
Melissa Mohr
Wendy Mok
Ray Moldenhauer
Helen Molton
Karen Momper
Ignacio Monge
Joe Montag
Angelo Montenegrino
Anna Montez
Mikael Monther
Jeff Montibeller
Katherine Montibeller
Quentin Montrie
Julia Montroy
Bernadette Moore
Jimmy Moore
Tracy Moore
Ruth Mora-Izturriaga
Teresa Morales
Lori Moran
Claudia Moreira
Valeria Moreno
Ivonne Moreno
Misty Morgan
Paul Morgan
Natascia Morgani
Larry Moritz

Elizabeth Morrison
Steve Morton
Nicola Morton
Jennifer Moser
Cathy Mosselman
Ivy Mouland House
Stelios Mourtzakis
Youssef Moussaoui
Rick Moy
Pierre Moyneur
Prasanta Mukherjee
Carl Mukri
Colin Mulholland
Christine Muller-Kekec
Sylvia Mullings
Paul Mullis
Lindsay Munn
Michael Murno
Jonathan Murphy
Austin Murray
Lorri Murray
Ruchiya Musikalak
Eda Mutlu
Joey Myers
Nahida Nabulsi
Paul Naecker
Nag Nagulapati
John Nagy
Yvonne Nagy
Atif Najmi
Thomas Nantka
Ismini Naos
Deepa Narayanan
Shashi Narayanan
Marcos Narvaez
Chris Naumann
Aungwara Nawacharoen
Armando Nazario
Handan Nazli
Ginger Neal
Sabine Nevermann
David Newman
Peter Newsham
Alan Ng
Vincent Ng
Jeffrey Ng
Dora Ng
Pauline Ng
Loc Nguyen
Doan Nguyen
Janice Nhan
Terence Nichols
Kevin Nickorick
Dorota Niedzwiecki
Kate Nigl
Neda Nikahd
David Nilsson
Wendy Niziol
Alan Noah-Navarro
Jonny Noble
Donna Noblin

Natalie Noel
Mickey Nojiri
Sara Noone
Corinna Nordin
Sutton Norris
Jessica Norsch
Sharon North
Martin Notzon
Douglas Noumbissi
Brandon Nuckelt
Martin Nunes
Erika Nunez
Edgar Nunnelly
Jason Oatis
Gyo Obata
Mark O'Brien
Erinn O'Brien
Jeanith Ocampo
Michael O'Con
Tim O'Connell
Kimberly O'Connor
Bill Odell
John Odom
William Ogle
Sang Hoon Oh
Pete Ohlhausen
Robert O'Keefe
Silvia Olar
Paola Oliva
Estelle Oliveri
Donovan Olliff
Mark Ondejko
Joseph O'Neill
James Ong
Jodie Ong
Sarah Oppenhuizen
Chuck Oraftik
Mary Orchard
Femi Oresanya
Mario Orofino
Breffni O'Rourke
Oswaldo Ortega
Arnold Ortiz
Marcela Ortiz
Adi Oruganti
Todd Osborne
Barbara Ostroff
Lou Oswald
Mark Otsea
Julia Ovsenni
Aneirin Owens
Milena Owsicka
Selin Ozertugrul
Eddie Pabon
Erika Pacheco
Judy Pack
Sharon Paculor
Manuel Padernos
Kristen Page
Hugh Painter
David Paisley

Bill Palmer
Tzveta Panayotova
Melissa Pantano
Stephen Papathopoulos
Manjiri Paprikar
Sharad Paranjape
Carter Paret
Sandra Paret
Chan Ho Park
Chansik Park
Minsik Park
Jiho Park
Gi-Young Park
Kate Park
Kevin Parks
Max Parsa
Chris Parshall
Steve Parshall
Melinda Parshall
Greg Parsons
Francisco Partida
Trelly Pascua
Jyoti Patel
Bharat Patel
Fenil Patel
Hitesh Patel
Nilesh Patel
Bill Patin
Stuart Patterson
Christopher Patterson
Nancy Paulsell
Elizabeth Pavlicek
Ant Payne
Jacqui Payne
Wendy Paz
Roberto Paz
Kristi Pearson
Ali Pedalino
Todd Pedersen
Mukang Pederson
Monica Pedroza
Talah Pejooh
Masha Pekurovsky
Shaney Pena Gomez
Clay Pendergrast Jr
Avanish Pendharkar
Arturo Peniche
Rutger Penick
Anthony Pent
Ian Pentland
Sharon Penttila
Eduardo Peon
Rhonda Perdue
Maaike Perenboom
Lankika Perera
Jill Perez
Amy Perez
Arturo Perez Rivera
Rollen Perry
Lars Pertwee
Renaldo Pesson

Deborah Pestell
Wade Peterson
Curtis Peterson
Caitlin Petschauer
Joe Pettipas
Bahram Pezeshki
Malika Phelps
Jincy Phillip
Amy Phillips
Scott Phillips
Stacey Phillips
Simon Phillips
Pallavi Phor
Van Phrasavath
Jason Pierce
Kevin Pierce
Craig Pierson
Brock Piglia
Jozef Pilasanovic
Dawn Pilgrim
Nihat Pilicer
Tony Pinelli
Tanja Pink
Michelle Pinkston
Donna Pipkins
Rosana Pirovano
Katya Piterman
Jesus Plata
Mike Plotnick
Michael Plumtree
Ryley Poblete
Angela Poe
Gian Luca Poggi
Jon Pohl
Tom Polucci
Antony Polyzotis
Brandon Poon
Amir Poonja
Felicia Pop
Forrest Popkin
Sam Poquiz
Andy Potter
Melissa Potts
Scott Powell
Dick Powers
Bob Powers
Natalia Pozdniakova
Jasmine Prachter
Anne Pradenas
Melissa Prado
Hernan Prado
Bob Pratzel
Kyle Prenzlow
Javier Presas
Mike Preston
Pamela Price
Scott Price
Travon Price
Simon Prichard
Ethan Primm
Bill Prindle

Derek Prior
Mark Pritchard
Rutha Prude
Michele Pruitt
Bonnie Przybyszewski
Lynn Puckett
Johnathan Puff
Jason Pugh
John Purcell
Janis Purgalis
Erik Purkey
Renee Purtle
Seven Qi
Monica Qing
Yen Quach
Thomas Quigley
David Quijano
Missy Quilizapa
Fergus Quinn
Greg Quintero
Patti Quiroz
Jeffery Raaphorst
Indra Arif Rachman
Jonathan Rae
Kamran Rafatian
Mamdouh Rafehi
Mariam Rafigh
Farhad Rahbary
Deepa Ramaswamy
Art Ramirez
Edgar Ramirez
Ronald Ramirez
Brandi Ramos
Sonia Ramundi
Eric Randall
Nageshwar Rao
Adam Rasmus
Ripley Rasmus
Leila Ray
Jamie Ray
Tony Raya
Marty Rayle
Chris Razzell
Theresa Rea
Alexander Redgrave
David Reese
Hossam Refaat
Mujib Rehman
Robert Reid
Russell Reid
John Reid
Valarie Reid
Susan Reimert
Jeffrey Rengering
Ellen Resurreccion
Gary Retel
Erika Reuter
Sandra Reyna
Jeff Reynolds
Jim Rice
Michael Rice

Diana Richards
Angela Richards
Cindy Richardson
Quinton Richardson
Monica Richmond
Lauren Ricks
Tracy Ried
Katie Rietz
Steve Riley
Sang Hun Rim
Matthew Rimstidt
Carmen Rinetzi
Mercy Rivas
Hernan Rivera
Michael Rivest
Alexander Robb
Stacy Robben
Abbey Roberson
Lance Roberts
Joe Robertson
Carolyn Robertson
Servillano Robes
Kimberly Robidoux
Tonisha Robinson
David Robinson
Daphne Robinson
Sean Robinson
Amanda Robinson
Barry Robinson
Tiera Robinson
Teresa Robinson
Tom Robson
Marty Rocca
Stephanie Rocha
Richard Rodgers III
Fernando Rodrigues
Reshma Rodrigues
Adriana Rodriguez
Macrina Rodriguez
Peter Rodriguez
Felix Rodriguez
Alex Rodriguez
Sara Rodriguez
Shelly Roebuck-Joseph
Anthony Roesch
Will Roess
Tom Roessler
William Roger
Tim Rogers
Stephanie Rogers
Colin Rohlfing
Kristen Rohrer
Cara Rolufs
Eric Romano
Rajinder Rooprai
Amy Roots
Scott Rose
Genevieve Rose
Mark Rosen
Lyn Rosenberg-Johnson
Carl Ross

Joshua Roth
Kylie Roth
Danny Rothe
Mathew Roush
Michel Rousseau
Jessica Rowen
Mark Rowlands
Rebecca Rowney
Darcy Royalty
Liz Royzman
David Rozzi
Sibylle Ruefenacht
Michael Ruiz
Paulina Ruiz
Nello Rusca
David Rush
Isaac Rush
Zach Rushing
Donny Russell
Bryon Russell
Michael Russo
Teresa Russo
Patryk Ruszkowski
Deborah Rutherford
Jeff Ryan
Chris Ryan
Mary Sabel
Maha Sabra
Mitchell Sahagian
Kibur Sahlu
Scott Saikley
Fariba Sajabi
Zaid Saleh
Dave Salela
Edward Salgian
Gian Carlo Salonga
Carmine Sampogna
Nathan Sampson
Mark Sams
Chris Sams
Pamela Sams
Nibu Samuel
Brian Sanchez
Fabiola Sanchez
Luis Sanchez
Anna Sandberg
Sara Sanders
Ivan Sandoval
Robert Sannella
Jeff Sanner
Jason Santeford
Olivier Santoni-Costantini
Jan Santos
Yiselle Santos
Daniele Santos
Richard Saravay
Brion Sargent
M S Sarupiyan
Rie Sasaki Gomes
Meiko Sato
Mark Sauer

Joyce Saunders	Manish Sharma	Paul Smead	Cheryl Steffe	Pei Ju Tai
Matthew Saunders	Shruti Sharma	Jeremy Smith	Lindsay Steffes	Jim Takagi
Meredith Savage	Donna Sharpe	Douglas Smith	Phillip Steffy	Jacqueline Tam
Jayson Savino	Nadia Shattler	Michael Smith	Julie Stein	Janice Tam
Rohit Saxena	Steven Shaw	Rich Smith	Jeffrey Steiner	Jesie Tan
Butch Sayson	Joseph Shaw	Don Smith	Archie Stephens	Christopher Tan
Thomas Scarda	Jeremy Shaw	Jim Smith	Luke Stephens	Kiajoon Tan
Mark Schaffhausen	Elina Shchervinsky	Ron Smith	James Stephens	Marco Tandoi
Maya Schali	Michele Sheehan	Steve Smith	Mike Stern	Ke Tang
Jeff Schantz	Roshanak Sheikhrezai	Charles Smith	Julie Stewart	Fanny Tang
Eric Schappe	Eric Shelton	Greg Smith	Julie Stewart	Marissa Tan-Gatue
David Scheck	Jessica Shen	Akash Smith	Bill Stinger	Helen Tannock
Peter Schefcick	Katie Shepherd	Greg Smith	Brittany Stinger	George Tanunagara
Vincent Schell	Kim Shepherd	Leanna Smith	Stan Stinnett	Sal Tappuni
Michele Schellhardt	Shauna Shepston	Matt Smith	Steve Stock	Josiane Tardif
Lelia Scheu	Melody Shi	Tim Smith	Kim Stockton	Scott Taricco
Gisela Schmidt	Sally-Yuan Yuan Shi	Shushana Smith	Darien Stokes	Donald Tate
Patrick Schmidt	Kayo Shibano	Henry Smith	Emillio Stokes	Jay Tatum
Laura Schmidt	Chisato Shimada	Lori Smith	Scott Stolarz	Jacqueline Tay
Falynn Schmidt	Kaoru Shimada	Ashley Smith	Crystal Stone	Tiffany Tay
Travis Schmiesing	Satomi Shimamura	Barry Smith	Paul Strain	Donald Taylor
Melissa Schmitz	Elizabeth Shipley	Brian Smyth	Gordon Stratford	Alicia Taylor
Kate Schmitz	Callie Shockley	Matt Snelling	Neil Stratford	Jamie Taylor
Lori Schneider	Julie Shon	Wayne Snyder	Kevin Strayer	Tatjana Taylor
Kean Schultheis	Freni Shroff	Jason Chi Wai So	Sasha Strickland	Seth Teel
Jillian Schultz	Dganit Shtorch	Ricardo Socorro	Wayne Striker	Karen Temple
Sheryl Schulze	Boris Shtykan	Theresa Solari	Leigh Stringer	David Teng
Louis Schump	Kevin Shumbera	Veda Solomon	Paul Strohm	Anna Tennent
Roger Schwabacher	Brett Shwery	Aya Solomyanik	Jeff Strohmeyer	Matthew Tether
Andrew Schwabe	Nicolas Sibal	Bokki Son	Nekia Strong	Sameer Thadikkaranthakth
David Schwartz	Chuck Siconolfi	Byung Eon Song	Meredith Strout	Sam Theye
Bob Schwartz	Ieva Sidaraite	Kwang Hyun Song	Matthew Stuart	Michael Thoma
Drew Scoggin	Tarver Siebert	Janet Wan Wen Song	Marti Stubblefield	Justin Thomas
Somer Scott	Anna Sigler	Roger Soto	Robert Studd	Stephen Thomas
Mano Scott	Christina Sigliano	Mona Soto	Sue Su	Tracy Thomas
Paul Scovill	Carol Silch	Scott Southerland	Hua Su	Stephen Thomas
Michele Scurry	Felipe Silva	Anthony Spagnolo	Vishal Sukhi	Tom Thomas
Francis Sebastian	Francisco Silva	Ton Span	Soran Sulaiman	Scott Thompson
Darko Sefic	Chris Silverberg	Neal Spanier	Kyle Sullivan	Barbara Thompson
Jeannette Segal	Jerry Silverman	Stephanie Spann	Suren Sumian	Jeannette Thompson
Joseph Seguin	Carolina Simon	Sam Spata	Rebecca Summers	Vance Thompson
John Seitz	Esther Simon	Julie Spencer	Hao Sun	Sheri Thompson
Roger Sekol	Alyssa Simons	Richard Spencer	Sam Sunada	Shaun Thomsen
Lori Selcer	Tommy Sinclair	Deborah Sperry	Sihyun Sung	Charlotte Thomsen
Jessie Self	Ayanna Sinclair	Rachel Spieczny	Adry Suryadi	Christine Thrash
Stacy Sensel	Sumati Singh	Niles Spiro	Barry Sutherland	Hong Tian
Manny Serrano	Vani Singh	Heather Spithoff	Charmaine Sutton	Rob Tibbetts
Alida Sertthin	Andy Singletary	Adam Spitz	Liz Sutton	Han Tieu
Barry Sewal	Nishu Sinha	Kristin Spradley	Zafer Suzer	Maureen Tighe
Kevin Sexton	Meagan Sinn	Renee Sprunger	Ben Suzuki	Chris Timmerman
Ami Shah	Ali Sirajuddin	Modesty St. John	Jon Svehla	Diana Tiron
Kartik Shah	Rim Siris	Kyle St. Peter	Kaven Swan	Ross Tisdale
Urvashi Shah	Lily Siu	Mike Stagner	Matthew Sweig	Mike Tobriner
Saurin Shah	Patricia Siu	Rachel Stanford	Kim Sydnor	Mike Tolleson
Sonal Shah	Sindu Sivayogam	Charlotte Stanske	Dan Sykes	Robin Tolud
Sejal Shah	Susan Skibell	Janice Stanton	Nancy Sylvio	Aneta Tomescu
Yusuf Shaikh	Nicholas Skinner	Aida Staugaard	Blair Symington	Christina Tonda
Robert Shakespeare	Jane Skulmoski	Adrienne Steadman	Galit Szolomowicz	Tat Yuen Tong
Dan Shan	Gregory Sledge	Nico Stearley	Julian Tablada	Kazem Toossi
Marie Shanks	Patrick Sloan	Melanie Steckel	Abdollah Tabrizi	Cecilia Toplikar
Erin Shanks	Steve Slosek	Julie Steele	Amer Taghlebi	Misa Torii

Elizabeth Torres
Ismael Torres
Vlad Torskiy
Steve Townsend
John Tran
Vu Tran
Phong Tran
Maria Tran
Kim Tran-Ngo
Jennifer Trevino
Sylvia Trevino
Silvia Trigueros
Patsy Trine
Hong Trinh
Dave Troup
Chris Trowbridge
Natasha Troy
Shelley True
Nancy Tsai
Wayne Tseng
Sara Tsiropinas
Larry Tsoi
Norman Tsui
Annie Tsui
Mark Tubello
Brey Tucker
Megan Tuite
Randa Tukan
Alex Tunik
Kent Turner
Caitlin Turner
Sharon Turner
Nita Tuvesson
Caroline Twombly
Sean Twomey
Tim Tynan
Michael Tynan
Reena Ubaid
Hardik Udani
Derek Ullian
Jason Ulrich
Mitchell Ulrich
Tim Ulrich
Jessica Uman
Walter Urbanek
Tania Ursomarzo
Karen Vaccarello
Sandy Valentin
Bill Valentine
Mike Valenzuela
Jamila Valero
Elizabeth Van Derbeck
Bob van Ermel Scherer
Christiaan Van Goolen
Yolanda Van Hecke
Michelle Van Kuijk
Bart Van Vliet
Louie Vargas
Jesus Vargas
Alex Vartanian
Jalpa Vasani

Fred Vasquez
Anna Vasquez
Valerie Vaughn
David Vazquez
Mariana Vega
Edmund Velasco
Mary Vella
Paul Velluet
Prithi Venkatram
Frank Vento
Marissa Venturo
Ignacio Vera
Andres Vergara
Israel Vergara
Reuben Verkamp
Joseph Vickery
Amanda Vidler
Ricardo Villagomez
Hilda Villavicencio
Rachel Villnow
Lioudmila Viltchek
Kim Vinson
Mimi Violette
Nalinee Viriyachai
Casey Visintin
Mark Vogl
John Vogt
Eva Von Huff
Amy Vonderau
Adriaan Vorster
Evgeny Voutchkov
Alicia Wachtel
Christine Waggener
Allison Wagner
Jason Wah
Bill Wahle
Daniel Wahlig
Deborah Waitzman
Nicole Walden
Jason Walker
Miles Walker
Christy Wallace
Debra Wallace
Dena Walter
Claire Walter
Julie Walters
Scott Walzak
Jason Wandersee
Yan Wang
Kyle Wang
Rain Wang
Michael Wang
Esther Wang
Fang Wang
Keanu Wang
Mabel Wang
Sam Ward
Quincy Wargo
Jana Warnatzsch
Connie Warner
Gene Warren

Jeffrey Warren
Tara Wasmuth
La Creta Waters
Nick Watkins
Paul Watson
Angie Watson
Wendy Wattam
Mateusz Wawrzyniak
Ken Webb
Stacy Webb
Melissa Webb
Evan Webber
Sinclair Webster
Jean Weiss-Bartelli
Sarah Weissman
Cheryl Welch
Bin Weng
Joe Werla
Doug West
Anna Wex
Tim Weyand
Yann Weymouth
Emma Wharton
Bill Wheeler
Kirsten Wheeler
Paul Whelan
Ryan Whitacre
Diana White
Claire Whitehill
David Whiteman
Larry Whitlock
Agatha Wieczorek
Sue Wiest
Alissa Wiggins
Lisa Wilbanks
Wayne Wilcox
John Wilganowski
Ryan Wilhelm
Paul Wilhelms
Clair Wilkinson
Marta Willgoose
Savannah Williams
Kevin Williams
Courtney Williams
Ken Williams
Brigitte Williams
Lou Williams
Brenda Williams
Makiea Williams
Sean Williams
Jodi Williams
Lisa Williams
Morgan Williams
Carla Williams
Claire Williams
Richard Williams
Jane Williams
Matt Wilson
Monte Wilson
Jim Wilson
Leslie Wilson

Ryan Wilson
Glenn Wing
Hank Winkelman
Richard Winokur
Re'ut Winter
Pete Winters
Joe Winters
John Witherspoon
Peggy Withrow
Steve Witte
Brandon Wojcik
Monika Wojtasik
Terrie Wolff
Meredith Wollman
Nicole Wolven
Seong Won
Wa Wong
Belinda Wong
Sylvester Wong
Daniel Wong
Yau Ng (Danny) Wong
Jones Wong
Mary Wong
Raymond Wong
Teresa Wong
Winnie Wong
Jeffrey Wong
Lewis Wong
Hayley Wood
Mike Woods
Polly Woods
Joseph Woods
Paul Woolford
Jeffrey Wotowiec
Melody Wright
Nick Wright
Eddie Wu
Meghan Wunderlich
Helen Wylie
Tai Xi
Lin Xia
Sam Xiong
Jin Xu
Nibras Yacoub
Junko Yamakawa
Todd Yamanouchi
Nicholas Yan
Jae Yan
Charlies Yang
Wendy Yang
Ken Yang
Joe Yang
Hyun-Joon Yang
Sala Yao
Yi Ting Yau
Stephanie Yearwood
Helen Yee
Robel Yemane
Justina Yeo
Wendy Yeung
Kelly Yeung

Lydia Yeung
Zehra Yilmaz
Cheong Wai Ken Yim
Suhyun Yim
Raymon Yim
Steven Yin
Sue Yin
Katherine Yip
Suk Yiu
Luke Yoo
SungJun Yoon
Jeff York
Heesik Youn
Ken Young
Belinda Young
Al Younkin
Yong Yu
Minggao Yu
Yuan Yuan
Louis Yuen
Grace Yuen
Cristina Yulo
Ashraf Yunus
Wesam Zaghmout
Michael Zajkowski
Antonio Zamora
Irena Zamozniak
Tom Zapoticzny
Damaso Zarate
Justin Zawyrucha
Sirine Zeitoune
Carmela Zenarosa
Julie Zeng
Bing Zeng
Daisy Zhai
Xin Zhang
Yang Zhang
Monica Zhang
Cynthia Zhang
Jie Zhang
Tracy Zhao
Tan Zheng
Jade Zheng
Dan Zhou
Joe Zhou
Yi Zhou
Alex Zhuang
Kirstin Ziemer
Laura Zimmerman
Connie Zinn
David Ziolkowski
Jason Zoss
Julijana Zrelec
Angela Zwink

HOK Global
Office Locations

UNITED STATES

Atlanta
191 Peachtree Street, NE, Suite 4100
Atlanta, GA 30303 USA
Voice +1 404 439 9000
Fax +1 404 439 9001

Chicago
60 East Van Buren Street, 14th Floor
Chicago, IL 60605 USA
Voice +1 312 782 1000
Fax +1 312 782 6727

Dallas
2711 North Haskell Avenue,
Suite 2250, LB 26
Dallas, TX 75204 USA
Voice +1 214 720 6000
Fax +1 214 720 6005

Denver
2190 East 17th Avenue
Denver, CO 80206 USA
Voice +1 303 832 1712
Fax +1 303 832 1713

Houston
2800 Post Oak Boulevard, Suite 3700
Houston, TX 77056 USA
Voice +1 713 407 7700
Fax +1 713 407 7809

Los Angeles
9530 Jefferson Boulevard
Culver City, CA 90232 USA
Voice +1 310 838 9555
Fax +1 310 838 9586

Miami
180 NE 39th Street, Suite 218
Miami, FL 33137 USA
Voice +1 786 497 4810
Fax +1 786 497 4811

New York
620 Avenue of the Americas, 6th Floor
New York, NY 10011 USA
Voice +1 212 741 1200
Fax +1 212 633 1163

San Francisco
One Bush Street, Suite 200
San Francisco, CA 94104 USA
Voice +1 415 243 0555
Fax +1 415 882 7763

St. Louis
211 North Broadway, Suite 700
St. Louis, MO 63102 USA
Voice +1 314 421 2000
Fax +1 314 421 6073

Tampa
One Tampa City Center, Suite 1800
Tampa, FL 33602 USA
Voice +1 813 229 0300
Fax +1 813 223 7116

Washington, D.C.
Canal House, 3223 Grace Street, N.W.
Washington, DC 20007 USA
Voice +1 202 339 8700
Fax +1 202 339 8800

CANADA

Calgary
620 12th Avenue SW, Suite 400
Calgary, Alberta T2R 0H5 Canada
Voice +1 403 517 3888
Fax +1 403 517 3889

Ottawa
205 Catherine Street, Suite 101
Ottawa, Ontario K2P 1C3 Canada
Voice +1 613 226 9650
Fax +1 613 226 9656

Toronto
720 King Street West, Suite 505
Toronto, Ontario M5V 2T3 Canada
Voice +1 416 203 9993
Fax +1 416 203 9992

Vancouver
1085 Homer Street, Suite 330
Vancouver, British Columbia V6B 1J4
Canada
Voice +1 604 648 1068
Fax +1 604 648 1069

LATIN AMERICA

Mexico City
Paseo de la Reforma 265, MZ1
Colonia Cuauhtémoc, 06500 México, DF
Voice +52 55 5208 0801
Fax +52 55 5208 0802

EUROPE

London
Qube
90 Whitfield Street
London W1T 4EZ
United Kingdom
Voice +44 0 20 7636 2006
Fax +44 0 20 7636 1987

ASIA PACIFIC

Beijing
Unit 1705, 17/F China Resources Building
No. 8 Jianguo Menbei Avenue
Beijing 100005 PR China
Voice +8610 8519 2898
Fax +8610 8519 2899

Hong Kong
24/F Kinwick Centre 32 Hollywood Road
Central, Hong Kong
Voice + 852 2534 0000
Fax + 852 2534 0099

Shanghai
Suite 3705 A, Ciro's Plaza,
388 Nan Jing West Road
Shanghai, 200003 PR China
Voice +8621 6334 6181
Fax +8621 6334 6182

Singapore
100 Beach Road, #16–08 Shaw Tower
Singapore, 189702
Voice +65 6291 1911
Fax +65 6396 0600

MIDDLE EAST

Dubai
P.O. Box 26437, 1501 API World Tower,
Sheikh Zayed Road
Dubai, UAE
Voice + 971 4 332 9116
Fax + 971 4 332 9117

INDIA

Mumbai
Design and Planning Services (India) Pvt Ltd
Voice +91 98 33 24864

Photography and
Illustration Credits

40 Peak Road Residential Development
Kerun Ip (1, 3–5)

150 California
Nick Merrick (1–5, 7)

Accenture Offices
Nick Merrick – Hedrich Blessing

AGL Resources Headquarters Renovation
Gabriel Benzur

Alfred A. Arraj United States Courthouse
Greg Hursley (1, 5)
Frank Ooms (2, 3, 4)

Allsteel Resource Center Showroom and Offices
Hedrich Blessing (1, 3, 4)

America Online Regional Headquarters
Benny Chan (1, 2)
Scott McDonald (3, 4)

Amsterdam Passenger Terminal
Christian Richters

Anaheim Convention Center
Timothy Hursley (2–4)

Barclays Bank Headquarters
David Churchill (1, 3, 4, 6, 8)
Peter Cook (7)

**Barnes-Jewish Hospital
Center for Advanced Medicine**
Timothy Hursley (1, 2, 4, 5)

Barranca del Muerto 329
Hector Velasco

Biogen Idec Campus
Scott McDonald (2, 4)

Bladensburg High School
Michael Dersin (1, 2)
Alan Karchmer (3, 4)

Boeing Leadership Center Campus and Carriage House
Steve Hall – Hedrich Blessing (1, 3–5)
Courtesy Boeing (2)

Capital One Canada Offices
Tom Arban

**Central Japan International Airport
(Chubu Centrair) Terminal**
SS Inc. (1, 3–5)

Chevy Chase Center
Joseph Romeo

Children's Discovery Museum
Sonny Boyden

Cisco Systems Executive Briefing Center
David Wakely

Ciudad Mitras Master Plan
David Carrico

Community Hospital of the Monterey Peninsula
Lawrence Anderson (2)

Community of Christ World Headquarters
Balthazar Korab

**Confluence Greenway and Great Rivers
Greenway Master Plan**
Photographers Direct/Skyscan/© J. Wark (2)

Cork International Airport Passenger Terminal
Gerry O'Leary

**The Darwin Centre Phase One
at The Natural History Museum**
Peter Durant (1, 3–5)

Dasve Village Master Plan, Lavasa Hill Station
David Carrico (1, 5)

Dechert LLP Law Offices
David Barbour

Dubai Marina Master Plan
Tom Arban (1, 3–5)

East Taihu Lake Waterfront District
Crystal Computer Graphics

Edificio Malecon Office Tower
Daniela Mac Adden (1–3, 5)

Emerson Grand Basin / *Post-Dispatch* Lake in Forest Park
Saint Louis Art Museum, Museum purchase, 1916 (2)

**Federal Reserve Bank of Cleveland Headquarters
Expansion and Renovation**
Timothy Hursley (1, 3–5)

**Federal Reserve Bank of Minneapolis
Headquarters and Operations Center**
Don Wong

Florida Aquarium
George Cott

**Florida International University
Patricia & Philip Frost Art Museum**
John Gillan (1, 3, 7)

Foreign & Commonwealth Office, Whitehall
Peter Cook (1, 2, 4)
Adam Woolfitt (3)

40 Grosvenor Place
Peter Cook (1–3, 6)

Franchise Tax Board Offices
John Swain (1)

**Fukuoka International Airport
International Passenger Terminal**
Tim Griffith

Georgia Archives
Timothy Hursley (3–5)

Guy Carpenter Headquarters
Peter Paige

Hampton Roads Convention Center
John Lesko (4)
Alan Karchmer (5)

Indianapolis International Airport
Col. H. Weir Cook Terminal
Sam Fentress (1, 3, 4)

James J. Stukel Towers and UIC Forum –
University of Illinois
James Steinkamp (3, 4)

JWT Offices
Michelle Litvin

Kellogg Corporate Headquarters
William Mathis (2, 3)

Kent County Courthouse
Adrian Wilson

Kiener Plaza
Designers: Rollin Stanley, Johann Hommel (1–6)

Killbear Provincial Park Visitor Centre
Tom Arban

King's Library at the British Museum
James Brittain

Kingwood College Health & Science Building
Joe Aker

London Marriott West India Quay Tower
David Churchill (2–5)
Nicholas Kane (6)

Maricopa County Fourth Avenue Jail
Tim Griffith (1, 2)

MasterCard Global Technology
and Operations Headquarters
Chris Barrett – Hedrich Blessing

McGuire Woods LLP Law Offices
Scott McDonald

MedImmune Research and Office Campus
Ron Solomon (1, 4, 5)

Missouri Historical Society
Expansion and Renovation
Robert Pettus (1)
Balthazar Korab (2, 3, 4)

Motorola Executive Offices Renovation
Chris Barrett

National Air and Space Museum
George Silk (2–5)

National Air and Space Museum
Steven F. Udvar-Hazy Center
Joseph Romeo (1, 3)
Alan Karchmer (4)
Elizabeth Lui (5, 6, 7, 8)

National Wildlife Federation Headquarters
Alan Karchmer (2)

Nortel Brampton Centre
Richard Johnson (1)
Chas McGrath (2)

Ogilvy & Mather Offices
Michelle Litvin (1, 3, 4)

One McKinley Place
Kerun Ip (1, 2)

Orange County Groundwater Replenishment System
Lawrence Anderson

The Priory Chapel
George Silk (2–6)

Reforma 27 Tower
Jesus Vargas

St. Barnabas Church
Peter Cook

St. George Intermodal and Cultural Center
Adrian Wilson (2, 4)

Salvador Dali Museum
Opiflex Architectural Imagery (1, 3, 5)

Sam M. Gibbons U.S. Courthouse
George Cott

Samsung Research and Development Campus
Jae Kyeong Kim

San Bernardino Natural Sciences Annex
California State University
John Edward Linden

San Mateo County Sheriff's Forensic
Laboratory and Coroner's Office
Cesar Rubio

Sanya Haitang Bay National Seashore Master Plan
Chris Battersby (1)
Xpgoo Computer Graphics Technology Co. Ltd. (2)

Sheraton Timika Eco-Hotel
Nick Merrick – Hedrich Blessing

SJ Berwin LLP Offices
Peter Cook

Symantec Executive Boardroom
David Wakely

Time Inc. Conference Center
Peter Paige

Tokyo Telecom Center
Timothy Hursley (2–4)

Tyson Foods Discovery Center
Sam Fentress

University Health Network Toronto Hospital
New Clinical Services Building
Robert Burley – Design Archives (1)
David Whittaker (2)

The University of Houston-Clear Lake
Student Services Building
Joe Aker

U.S. Department of State Nairobi Embassy Compound
Elizabeth Lui

U.S. Department of State New Office Building
Alan Karchmer

U.S. EPA Environmental Research Center
Alan Karchmer (1–5)

USAA Phoenix Norterra Campus
Hedrich-Blessing (1, 2, 3, 5)

Warner Music Canada Headquarters
Ben Rahn (1–3)

William Rainey Harper College Avanté Center
Paul Rivera (1, 3, 4)

WilTel Technology Center Headquarters
Timothy Hursley (1, 2, 4)
Scott McDonald – Hedrich Blessing (3)

Winrock International Headquarters
Craig Dugan

Zayed University
Alan Karchmer (2, 3, 4, 8)

Zentrum Tower
Hector Velasco